Instant Pot Duo Nova
Air Fryer Lid Cookbook 2020-2021

The Easy Tendercrispy Recipes for Any 6-Quart Instant Pot Multi-Use Programmable Pressure Cooker with Air Fryer Lid

By Danny Cookery

Warning-Disclaimer

The purpose of this book is to educate and entertain. The author or publisher does not guarantee that anyone following the techniques, suggestions, tips, ideas, or strategies will become successful. The author and publisher shall have neither liability or responsibility to anyone with respect to any loss or damage caused, or alleged to be caused, directly or indirectly by the information contained in this book.

Contents

Description...1

Introduction..2

Chapter 1: Instant Pot Duo Nova Air Fryer Lid 101....................... 3

What is Instant Pot Duo Nova Air Fryer Lid?............................... 3
Components of Instant Pot Duo Nova Air Fryer Lid................... 4
Functions of Instant Pot Duo Nova Air Fryer Lid....................... 7
How does it work.. 9
Cleaning and Maintenance of Instant Pot Duo Nova Air
Fryer Lid.. 10

Chapter 2: Tips for Usage of Instant Pot Duo Nova Air Fryer.....11

**Chapter 3: Common FAQs for Instant Pot Duo Nova Air Fryer
Lid...12**

Chapter 4: Breakfast Recipes...13

Baked Eggs... 13
Breakfast Souffle... 15
Egg Muffins... 16
Cinnamon Toast.. 17
Egg Casserole... 18
Sausage, Eggs and Cheese Mix..19
Breakfast Egg Bowls...20
Biscuits Casserole... 21
Creamy Hash Browns..22
Asparagus Frittata..23

Chapter 5: Red Meat Recipes...24

Oriental Air Fried Lamb...24
Short Ribs and Special Sauce... 26
Roasted Pork Belly and Apple Sauce......................................27

Lemon Glazed Lamb...28
Creamy Ham and Cauliflower.. 29
Instant Air Fried Sausage and Mushrooms.....................30
Sausage and Kale Soup.. 31
Sirloin Steaks and Pico De Gallo....................................32
Coffee Flavored Steaks..34
Beef Kabobs...35

Chapter 6: Poultry Recipes...36

Honey Duck Breasts...36
Chicken and Parsley Sauce.. 37
Chicken and Green Onions Sauce.................................39
Baked Greek Chicken... 40
Cider-Glazed Chicken... 41
Turkey, Peas, and Mushroom Casserole.........................42
Chicken Tenders and Flavored Sauce...........................43
Chicken and Radish Mix... 44
Chicken Breast with Passion Fruit Sauce........................45
Duck and Plum Sauce...46

Chapter 7: Seafood Recipes... 47

Instant Air Fried Branzino... 47
Marinated Salmon..48
Hawaiian Salmon...49
Chinese Cod.. 50
Halibut and Sun-Dried Tomatoes Mix............................ 51
Stuffed Calamari..52
Crusted Salmon...53
Swordfish and Mango Salsa.. 54
Squid and Guacamole..55
Tuna and Chimichurri Sauce...57

Chapter 8: Soups, Stews, and Broths.............................59

Creamy Chicken Stew..59

Chicken Consommé..61
Tofu Vegetable Soup...62
Greek Egg and Lemon Soup..63
Chive Vichyssoise...64
White Borscht...65
Chunky Seafood Chowder...66
Gingered Tofu and Noodle Soup...67
Minestrone...68
Hot, Hot Chili Soup...70

Chapter 9: Rice, Multi-grain, and Porridges.......................**72**
Rice, Almonds and Raisins Pudding......................................72
Rice and Sausage Side Dish...74
Blueberry and Brown Sugar Oatmeal...................................75
Wide Rice Pilaf...76
Pumpkin Rice..77
Wild Rice Soup...78
Rice Stuffed Bell Pepper Soup...80
Fresh Baked Oatmeal..81

Chapter 10: Beans, Chilis, and Eggs...................................**83**
French Beans and Egg Breakfast Mix...................................83
Chicken, Beans, Corn and Quinoa Casserole......................84
Green Beans Side Dish..85
Cod Fillets and Peas...86
Ham and Eggs..87
Egg White Chips...88
Scrambled Eggs...89
Fast Eggs and Tomatoes..90
Egg White Omelettes...91
Lunch Egg Rolls..92

Chapter 11: Vegetarian Recipes...**93**
Instant Air Fried Potato Chips...93

Delicious Air Fried Broccoli..94

Roasted Eggplant...95

Glazed Beets...96

Vermouth Mushrooms.. 97

Roasted Peppers...98

Creamy Brussels Sprouts and Ham.. 99

Garlic Potatoes...100

Chapter 12: Snacks and Desserts............................. 101

Sweet Potato Cheesecake.. 101

Cashew Bars...103

Mandarin Pudding...104

Sweet Squares..105

Figs and Coconut Butter Mix...106

Passion Fruit Pudding...107

Chocolate and Pomegranate Bars.......................................108

Blueberry Pudding..109

Chapter 13: Yogurt and Cake................................... 110

Tomato Cake...110

Tangerine Cake...111

Cauliflower Cakes...112

Ricotta and Lemon Cake.. 113

Maple Cupcakes..114

Lime Cheesecake...115

Chapter 14: Slow Cooking Recipes........................... 116

Seafood Chowder...116

Potatoes and Tomatoes Mix...118

Slow-Cooked Duck Breasts...119

Chinese Duck Legs...120

Balsamic Beef...121

Chapter 15: Sauté Recipes... 122

New England Haddock Chowder...122

Halibut Chowder...123
Filet Mignon and Mushroom Sauce...............................124
Simple Braised Pork.. 125
Instant Air-Fried Japanese Duck Breasts.......................127

Conclusion...**128**

Description

Crisp your meals to your heart's content with no hassle whatsoever!

Want to use an oven without actually having to buy one? The Instant Pot Duo Nova Air Fryer Lid is your answer. It is capable of performing all the functions of an oven and more. It doesn't stop there. The Air Fryer Lid completely excises the need for deep-frying your food. It makes use of 95% less oil and still gives you that even, crispy food texture you desire.

Why would you have to visit high-end restaurants or hotels to get the best? When you can prepare exquisite meals that rev up your hunger for more right in the comfort of your home. The Air Fryer Lid cooks food in such a way that the mouth-watering flavor, texture, and nutrients of the ingredients are retained and sometimes positively exacerbated. Although the Air Fryer lid can only cook for two to three people at a time, the speed at which it does so compensates for the small size; hence you can cook in batches and still be on time.

Meals cooked with the Instant Pot Air Fryer not only tastes heavenly, but they also look enticing. With the divine taste and the attractive looks of the dishes, the Instant Pot Duo Nova Air Fryer Lid is the right tool to make your cooking journey rewarding.

Introduction

The Instant Pot Air Fryer does not only substitute as an oven and a healthy deep-fryer, it dehydrates, broils, roasts, and also reheats cold food. All these can be achieved by merely switching your regular pressure lid with the Instant Pot Duo Nova Air Fryer Lid.

The Instant Pot Duo Nova Air Fryer Lid is purchased separately and is well-suited with all 6- quarts Instant Pot models only except; the Smart WiFi, Max, Duo SV, Duo Evo Plus, and Duo Evo Plus 6 models. The Instant Pot Air Fryer gives room for convenience, multi-tasking, customization as well as luxury in your meal preparations. This cookbook explains how to use the Instant Pot Duo Nova Air Fryer Lid and what to use it for to get your money's worth, your tummy's worth, and much more.

Let's dig in and get cooking!

Chapter 1: Instant Pot Duo Nova Air Fryer Lid 101

What is Instant Pot Duo Nova Air Fryer Lid?

The Instant Pot Pressure Cooker Lid comes together with the corresponding compatible Instant Pot Cooker Base. The autonomy of the Air Fryer lid stems from the fact that an Instant Pot Air Fryer can be used with a lot of different instant pot models, as earlier mentioned. It is independent of the restrictions attributed to custom-made Air Fryer lids (e.g., the Instant Pot Duo Crisp Lid) and also pressure cookers lids.

The Instant Pot Duo Nova Air Fryer Lid is a single kitchen appliance that not only complements the look of your kitchen, but it also makes you fall in love with cooking. It doesn't occupy space when in use and even when storing as it can comfortably lay in a kitchen cabinet or drawer. It is powered by electricity to produce hot air that cooks, fries, and crisps your meat, chicken, veggies, and desserts into finger-licking delicacies. With the single touch technology incorporated into its control panel, six smart food programs cook food at the range of 105 ° F-400 ° F cooking temperature. Quite a wide range, right?

The Instant Pot Duo Nova Air Fryer Lid is quite the unicorn in the Air Fryer universe.

Components of Instant Pot Duo Nova Air Fryer Lid

It is essential to know the components of the Instant Pot Duo Nova Air Fryer Lid and its functions. If you have them locked down, you will be able to use the Air fryer efficiently with little to no incidents.

➢ **Interior components**: The inner part of the air fryer lid comprises of the heating element (converts electrical energy into heat, which in this case is hot air) and the cover of the heating element.

➢ **Exterior components**: The outer part of the air fryer lid comprises of the handle, air intake and outlet vents, and the power cord that is plugged into an external electrical power source, preferably a wall socket.

> **Complementary components**: The Air Fryer is used together with other accessories to be functional. They include;

- Any compatible **Instant Pot cooker base** available to you.
- **A Stainless steel inner pot** is placed inside the cooker base when used.
- **Air Fryer Basket base** which is placed in the inner pot and sits the Air Fryer Basket.
- **Multi-level Air Fryer Basket** is used to hold the dehydrating tray or rack as the case may be.
- **The broil/dehydrating tray** is from stainless steel. Use a double-layered one if you are preparing for more than two people.

- **Protective pad/storage cover**: This accessory serves a dual purpose. It serves as a rest pad for a very hot, just unplugged, and detached Air Fryer lid. Alternatively, it serves as a protective cover once it has cooled. It protects the heating element from any unwanted external particles while it is in storage.

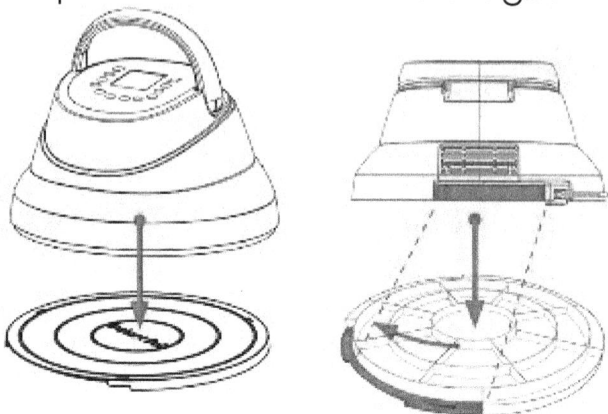

➢ **Single touch control panel**: this is the brain of the Air Fryer. It comprises of:

- **Start button**: push button to initiate the smart programs.
- **Cancel button** allows you to halt the smart running program at any time thereby, switching the Air Fryer Lid to standby mode.
- **Time and temperature buttons**: push the plus sign (+) to increase time and temperature and the minus sign (-) to reduce them.
- **Smart programs**: There are six food programs and six buttons. Each button has an LED indicator that indicates the food program is on. The programs are Air Fry, Broil, Bake, Roast, Reheat, and Dehydrate.
- **Display screen**: The screen displays the running cooking time and temperature, respectively. It also narrates the current state of the Air Fryer Lid. The status messages allow you to communicate with the Air Fryer. **Off** means the Lid is on standby mode, "**on**" means preheating has

commenced, **Lid** means either the Lid is not well placed, or the inner pot is missing. "**Turn food**" instructs you to flip the food. "**Cool**" means the appliance is cooling. "**End**" indicates the smart program has completed. "**Food burn**" means the inner pot is overheating.

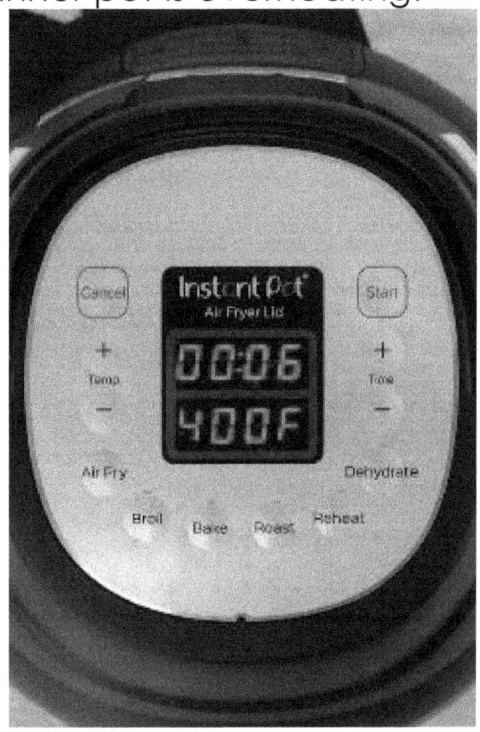

Functions of Instant Pot Duo Nova Air Fryer Lid

The primary services of the Instant Pot Duo Nova Air Fryer Lid are within the operations of the six smart programs as follows in the table below:

SMART PROGRAM	FUNCTION/EXAMPLES	ACCESSORY
AIR FRY	Thoroughly Cooks fresh food. Crisps already pressure cooked food. Defrosts food.	Air Fryer Basket

	For example, Beefsteak, Asparagus, Pork, Shrimps, chicken wings, and so on are Air Fried	
BROIL	It requires high temperature and very close proximity to heat. Grill meats and vegetables quickly to retain their flavor. Quite ideal for melting cheese on choice foods Fish, meat, cauliflower, broccoli, etc.	Broil tray, Air Fryer Basket
BAKE	It works like an oven to make snacks and desserts. For example, Cake, muffins, brownies, and most pastries use the bake-program.	Air Fryer Basket. Baking-Pan/Broil tray.
ROAST	Crisps skin of poultry, meat, pork until they are crunchy. It gives food an appealing golden brown coloration.	Air Fryer Basket.
REHEAT	Works as a microwave to warm food and still retain moisture without overcooking	Air Fryer Basket. Broil/dehydrating tray Oven-safe baking pan.
DEHYDATE	Synonymous with pressure cooking slow cook. It requires low heat and long cooking time. It extracts moisture from food	Air Fryer Basket Broil/dehydrating tray

| | for preservation.
Can make Vegetable chips,
meat jerky, fruit leather, etc. | |

How does it work

The following steps explain how the Instant Pot Duo Nova Air Fryer Lid typically works:

- First, ensure the Instant Pot Cooker Base unplugged.
- Put your ingredients as required by the smart program, recipe, and food type.
- Attach the Air Fryer Lid (when you hear the customary locking tune of Instant Brand, you know it is locked in place). Plug into an electrical wall socket.
- Push the start button—the display screen shows "on" indicating the commencement of the preheating process.
- When the screen displays "turn food," remove the Lid and place it on a pad. Then, flip or stir the food using tongs or chopsticks.
- Reattach the Lid within three minutes to resume cooking.
- After the smart program completes, the screen displays "end," and the Lid makes a beep sound.
- You either remove the Air Fryer lid immediately to get to the food, or you leave the Lid for an additional one hour to keep the food warm.

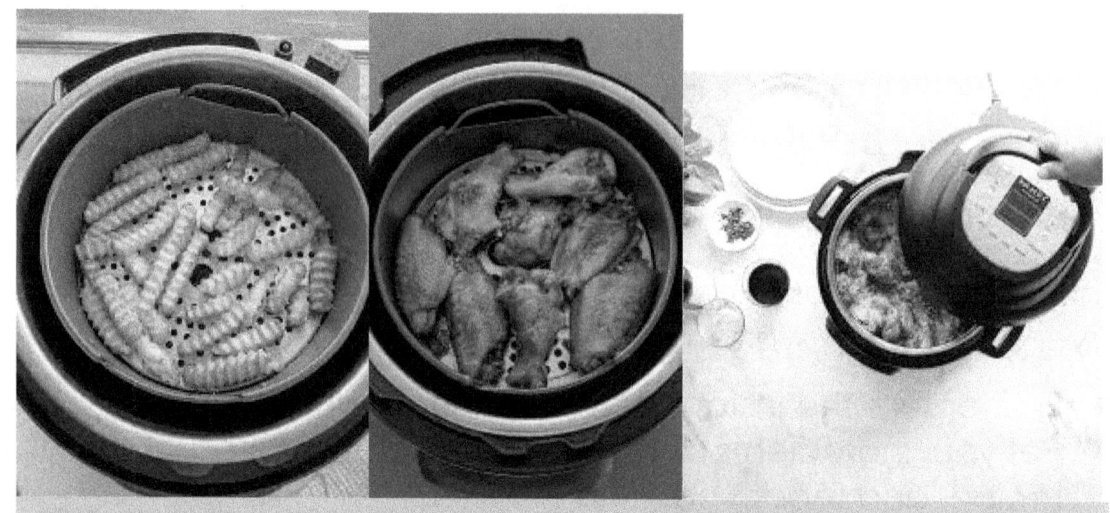

Cleaning and Maintenance of Instant Pot Duo Nova Air Fryer Lid

Regular cleaning and maintenance of the Instant Pot Duo Nova Air Fryer Lid are very crucial for its durability and hitch-free functionality.

- Always ensure all components are entirely cool (room temperature) before attempting and cleaning and maintenance efforts.
- To clean the Air Fryer lid, wet a soft rag and gently wipe away any debris or food particles on both the interior and exterior parts. Do not attempt to rinse or dip in the water. The power cord also requires the same treatment. Furthermore, folding the wire reduces its average life span.
- The complementary accessories excluding the cooker base can be hand washed with soap and water, preferably. However, a dishwasher also does the job.
- Once all are dried, pack away in a cool, dry space for storage.

Chapter 2: Tips for Usage of Instant Pot Duo Nova Air Fryer

Here a few tips to ensure an enjoyable experience with the Instant Pot Duo Nova Air Fryer Lid:

- After unboxing the appliance, the first course of action is to clean the Lid and all complimentary accessories to make sure there are no debris/particles from the packaging material.
- Plugging both the cooker base and the Air Fryer lid at the same time may lead to fire accidents and injury from electrical circuit overload.
- To reduce the number of food particles sticking to the Air Fry Basket, cover the bottom with either baking paper or aluminum foil before placing food in it.
- In addition to the customization of preset programs, the Instant Pot Duo Nova Air Fryer Lid also saves customized entries in the program memory after the start button is selected.

Chapter 3: Common FAQs for Instant Pot Duo Nova Air Fryer Lid

The following are adequate answers to some of your questions:

- **How to alter the default temperature scale?** First, ensure the Lid is on standby mode. Then, push and hold the plus sign on the temperature button until the temperature scale changes on the display screen.
- **How to put sound on and off?** Ensure the Lid is on standby mode. To put the alert-sound on, push and hold the plus sign on the time button until "SOn" is displayed. To put the alert-sound off, push and hold the minus sign on the time button until "SOFF" is displayed.
- **Why is the power cord so short?** It is a safety measure to ensure that no accidents and injuries are resulting from tripping, wire tangling, etc. that may occur if the cord was long.
- **What to do if I see black smoke coming from the Air Fryer lid?** This black smoke point to either a food burn event or the heating element is acting up. First, push the cancel button and remove the plug. Clean the appliance when cold. Splatters of food particles and oil might be the cause of the faulty heating element.
- **Is there a warranty for the appliance?** Yes. It comes with a twelve-month warranty starting from the precise date of purchase indicated in the receipt.

Chapter 4: Breakfast Recipes

Baked Eggs

This is an easy breakfast recipe that is perfected with the Instant Pot Duo Nova Air Fryer Lid. Try it now to understand the reason for the fuss.

Prep time and cooking time: 30 minutes | Serves: 4

Ingredients To Use:

- 4 medium eggs
- 1 Tbsp. of olive oil
- 1 pound of torn baby spinach
- 4 Tbsp. of milk
- 7 ounces of chopped ham
- Salt and black pepper, as desired
- Cooking spray

Step-by-Step Directions to Cook It:

1. Heat the oil in a device compatible with the Instant Pot Duo Nova Air Fryer Lid, then add the baby spinach and cook until tender.
2. Coat 4 ramekins with the cooking spray and fill it up with the ham and cooked baby spinach.
3. Add an egg to each ramekin, 1 Tbsp. of milk, and season with salt and pepper.
4. Transfer the ramekins to an oven-safe baking dish and place it in the Instant Pot cooker base.
5. Position the broil/dehydration tray, and cover with the Instant Pot Duo Nova Air Fryer Lid.

6. Select the Bake Smart Program and adjust the time and temperature to 20 minutes and 350°F, respectively. Select *Start* to begin baking.
7. Serve for Breakfast.

Nutritional value per serving:

Calories: 321kcal, Fat: 6g, Carbs: 15g, Protein: 12g

Breakfast Souffle

A very light dish perfect for mornings. It is stress-free and can be prepared within 20 minutes.

Prep time and cooking time: 18 minutes | Serves: 4

Ingredients To Use:

- 1 medium onion, diced
- 4 Tbsp. of heavy cream
- 4 medium eggs, whisked
- A pinch of red chili pepper, crushed
- 2 Tbsp. of chopped chives
- 2 Tbsp. of chopped parsley + 1 tsp. to garnish
- Salt and black pepper, as desired

Step-by-Step Directions to Cook It:

1. Mix the eggs, salt, black pepper, red chili pepper, onion, parsley, heavy cream, and chives in a medium bowl. Whish thoroughly.
2. Transfer the mixture to 4 soufflé dishes and arrange in the Instant Pot cooker base.
3. Fit the Instant Pot Duo Nova Air Fryer Lid and select the Bake Smart Program. Adjust the time to 8 minutes and the temperature to 350°F—select *Start* to begin.
4. Remove, garnish with parsley, and serve immediately.

Nutritional value per serving:

Calories: 300kcal, Fat: 7g, Carbs: 15g, Protein: 6g

Egg Muffins

Muffins are easy to prepare and always ready to save the day. Try this recipe out now with the Instant Pot Duo Nova Air Fryer Lid to understand the real meaning of scrumptious.

Prep time and cooking time: 25 minutes | Serves: 4

Ingredients To Use:

- 1 medium egg
- 2 Tbsp. of olive oil
- 3 Tbsp. of milk
- 3.5 ounces of white flour
- 1 Tbsp. of baking powder
- 1/2 cup of diced baby spinach
- 1 cup of yellow onion
- 1 cup of diced red and green pepper
- 2 ounces of grated parmesan
- A splash of Worcestershire sauce

Step-by-Step Directions to Cook It:

1. Mix the egg, flour, baking powder, baby spinach, bell pepper, oil, milk, Worcestershire sauce, and parmesan. Whisk thoroughly and serve into 4 muffin cups.
2. Transfer the cup to the air fryer and cover with the Instant Pot Duo Nova Air Fryer Lid.
3. Select the Bake Smart Program and adjust the time to 15 minutes and the temperature to 392°F
4. Serve immediately.

Nutritional value per serving:

Calories: 251kcal, Fat: 6g, Carbs: 9g, Protein: 3g

Cinnamon Toast

Eat your toast crunchy and tasty with this cinnamon recipe.

Prep time and cooking time: 15 minutes | Serves: 6

Ingredients To Use:

- 1 stick of soft butter
- 12 bread slices
- 1/2 cup of sugar
- 1-1/2 tsp. vanilla extract
- 1-1/2 tsp. cinnamon powder

Step-by-Step Directions to Cook It:

1. Mix the butter, sugar, cinnamon, and vanilla in a small bowl. Whisk thoroughly.
2. Spread the egg mixture on the bread slices and arrange them in the air fryer. Cover with the Instant Pot Duo Nova Air Fryer Lid and select the Bake Smart Program. Set the timer to 5 minutes and the temperature 400°F
3. Serve the bread.

Nutritional value per serving:

Calories: 221kcal, Fat: 4g, Carbs: 12g, Protein: 8g

Egg Casserole

Taste the difference with this egg casserole recipe prepared with the Instant Pot Duo Nova Air Fryer Lid.

Prep time and cooking time: 35 minutes | Serves: 6

Ingredients To Use:

- 1 pound of ground turkey
- 1 Tbsp. of olive oil
- 1/2 tsp. of chili powder
- 12 medium eggs
- 1 sweet potato, cubed
- 1 cup of baby spinach
- Salt and black pepper, as desired
- 2 tomatoes, chopped for garnish

Step-by-Step Directions to Cook It:

1. Mix the eggs, salt, black pepper, sweet potato, turkey, chili powder, and spinach. Mix well.
2. Preheat the air fryer to 350°F, add the oil, then pour in the egg mix.
3. Spread the egg mix in the inner pot and cover with the Instant Pot Duo Nova Air Fryer Lid.
4. Select the Bake Smart Program and adjust the time to 25 minutes and the temperature to 350°F
5. Scrape the egg mix out of the air fryer and serve warm.

Nutritional value per serving:

Calories: 300kcal, Fat: 5g, Carbs: 13g Protein: 6g

Sausage, Eggs and Cheese Mix

This recipe is a perfect blend of sausages, eggs, and cheese. The egg holds the sausage together, and the cheese adds creaminess to the meal.

Prep time and cooking time: 30 minutes | Serves: 4

Ingredients To Use:

- 10 ounces of sausages, cooked and crumbled
- 1 cup of shredded cheddar cheese
- 1 cup of shredded mozzarella cheese
- 8 medium eggs, whisked
- 1 cup of milk
- Salt and black pepper, as desired
- Cooking spray

Step-by-Step Directions to Cook It:

1. Mix the sausages, mozzarella, cheddar, eggs, salt, black pepper, and milk in a small bowl.
2. Preheat the Instant pot air fryer to 380°F and add the eggs and sausage mixture. Cover with the Instant Pot Duo Nova Air Fryer Lid, Select the Bake Smart Program and adjust the time to 20 minutes.
3. Serve into plates.

Nutritional value per serving:

Calories: 320kcal, Fat: 6g, Carbs: 12g, Protein: 5g

Breakfast Egg Bowls

For mornings when you just want an easy recipe that can be prepared in a few minutes; this meal on the Instant Pot Duo Nova Air Fryer Lid has got you covered.

Prep time and cooking time: 30 minutes | Serves: 4

Ingredients To Use:

- 4 dinner rolls, tops cut off and insides scooped out
- 4 medium eggs
- 4 Tbsp. of heavy cream
- 4 Tbsp. of grated parmesan
- 4 Tbsp. mixed chives and parsley
- Salt and black pepper, as desired

Step-by-Step Directions to Cook It:

1. Arrange the dinner rolls on a flat surface, add an egg to each roll, then spice with the mixed herbs and heavy cream—season with salt and black pepper.
2. Add the parmesan to the rolls and transfer them to the inner pot of the Instant Pot Air Fryer.
3. Position the dehydration tray, cover with the Instant Pot Duo Nova Air Fryer Lid, and select the Bake Smart Program. Set the timer to 20 minutes and the temperature to 350°F. Click on Start to begin cooking.
4. Put each bread roll on a plate and serve.

Nutritional value per serving:

Calories: 238kcal, Fat: 4g, Carbs: 14g, Protein: 7g

Biscuits Casserole

Every bite comes with a unique combination of biscuit, sausages, and seasoning. The meal is healthy and highly delicious.

Prep time and cooking time: 25 minutes | Serves: 8

Ingredients To Use:

- 12 ounces of quartered biscuits
- 3 Tbsp. flour
- 1/2 pound of sausage, chopped
- A pinch of salt and black pepper
- 2-1/2 cup of milk
- Cooking spray

Step-by-Step Directions to Cook It:

1. Grease the inner pot of the air fryer with the cooking spray and preheat it to 350°F
2. Arrange the biscuits at the bottom of the pot, then layer it with the chopped sausage.
3. Mix the flour, salt, black pepper, and milk in a bowl, then transfer it to the inner pot. Cover with the dehydration tray and the Instant Pot Duo Nova Air Fryer Lid.
4. Select the Bake Smart Program and adjust the time to 15 minutes.
5. Serve immediately.

Nutritional value per serving:

Calories: 321kcal, Fat: 4g, Carbs: 12g, Protein: 5g

Creamy Hash Browns

Do you want to start your mornings like royalty? Then try this recipe out with the Instant Pot Duo Nova Air Fryer Lid, and you won't be disappointed.

Prep time and cooking time: 30 minutes | Serves: 6

Ingredients To Use:

- 2 pounds of hash browns
- 8 bacon slices, chopped
- 1 cup of whole milk
- 9 ounces of cream cheese
- 1 yellow onion, sliced
- 6 green onions, chopped
- 1 cup of shredded cheddar cheese
- 6 medium eggs
- Salt and black pepper, as desired
- Cooking spray

Step-by-Step Directions to Cook It:

1. Grease the inner pot of the air fryer with the cooking spray and preheat it to 350°F
2. Mix the eggs, milk, cheddar, cream cheese, onion, bacon, salt, and black pepper in a bowl. Whisk well.
3. Pour the hash browns and egg mix into the inner pot of the Instant Pot Air Fryer and cover with the Instant Pot Duo Nova Air Fryer Lid.
4. Select the Bake Smart Program and adjust the time to 20 minutes. Click Start to begin cooking.
5. Divide into equal portions and serve.

Nutritional value per serving:

Calories: 261kcal, Fat: 6g, Carbs: 8g, Protein: 12g

Asparagus Frittata

This is a lovely way to incorporate vegetables into your breakfast. With the Instant Pot Duo Nova Air Fryer Lid, you can eat healthily and deliciously.

Prep time and cooking time: 15 minutes | Serves: 2

Ingredients To Use:

- 4 medium eggs, whisked
- 2 Tbsp. parmesan, grated
- 4 Tbsp. milk
- Salt and black pepper, as desired
- 10 asparagus tips, steamed
- Cooking spray

Step-by-Step Directions to Cook It:

1. Grease the inner pot of the Instant Pot air fryer with the cooking spray and preheat it to 400°F
2. Mix the eggs, milk, parmesan, salt, and black pepper in a bowl. Whisk thoroughly and add the asparagus.
3. Transfer the asparagus egg mixture to the inner pot and cover with the Instant Pot Duo Nova Air Fryer Lid. Select the Bake Smart Program and cook for 5 minutes
4. Divide the frittata into equal portions and serve warm.

Nutritional value per serving:

Calories: 312kcal, Fat: 5 g, Carbs: 14g, Protein: 2g

Chapter 5: Red Meat Recipes

Oriental Air Fried Lamb

Here, the lamb is air fried for 8 minutes to improve the flavor and texture before adding to the stock.

Prep time and cooking time: 52 minutes | Serves: 8

Ingredients To Use:

- 2-1/2 pounds of chopped lamb shoulder
- 3 Tbsp. honey
- 3 ounces of chopped almonds, peeled
- 8 ounces of veggie stock
- 9 ounces of pitted plumps
- 2 yellow onions, chopped
- 1 tsp. cinnamon powder
- 2 garlic cloves, minced
- Salt and black pepper, as desired
- 1 tsp. ginger powder
- 1 tsp. cumin powder
- 1 tsp. turmeric powder
- 3 Tbsp. olive oil

Step-by-Step Directions to Cook It:

1. Preheat the Instant Pot to 350°F
2. Mix the cinnamon, ginger, turmeric, cumin, olive oil, garlic, and lamb. Ensure the lamb is adequately coated.
3. Transfer the seasoned lamb to the air fryer basket and cover it with Instant Pot Air Fryer Lid.

4. Select the Air Fry Smart Program and adjust the time to 8 minutes. You will be notified when it's time to *"Turn Food."*
5. Transfer the lamb to an oven-safe baking dish, add the onions, veggie stock, plums, and honey. Stir.
6. Cover with the Instant Pot Duo Nova Air Fryer Lid and cook for 35 minutes at 350°F
7. Divide into equal portions and serve.

Nutritional value per serving:

Calories: 332kcal, Fat: 23g, Carbs: 30g, Protein: 20g

Short Ribs and Special Sauce

The combination of spices and sauce in this recipe infuses flavor into the lamb. Each bite of the lamb will take you on an adventure to discover the cause of the rich flavor.

Prep time and cooking time: 46 minutes | Serves: 4

Ingredients To Use:

- 2 green onions, chopped
- 1 tsp. vegetable oil
- 3 garlic cloves, grated
- 3 ginger slices
- 1/2 cup of soy sauce
- 4 pounds of short ribs
- 1/2 cup of water
- 1/4 cup of pear juice
- 1/4 cup of rice wine
- 2 tsp. sesame oil

Step-by-Step Directions to Cook It:

1. Using the Instant Pot cooker base, select Sauté and heat the oil, then add the green onions, garlic, and ginger. Fry for a full minute, then press Cancel.
2. Add the wine, soy sauce, sesame oil, water, pear juice, and ribs to the inner pot.
3. Add the broil/dehydration tray, cover with the Instant Pot Duo Nova Air Fryer Lid, and select the Broil Smart Program. Set the timer for 30 minutes and the temperature for 350°F
4. Divide ribs into 4 portions and serve immediately.

Nutritional value per serving:

Calories: 321kcal, Fat: 12g, Carbs: 20g, Protein: 14g

Roasted Pork Belly and Apple Sauce

The lamb is coated with apple and lemon before roasting to allow for maximum absorption of flavor. The lemon gives the lamb a sharp, pleasant after taste.

Prep time and cooking time: 50 minutes | Serves: 6

Ingredients To Use:

- 2 Tbsp. sugar
- 1 quart of water
- 1 Tbsp. lemon juice
- 17 ounces of apples, cut into wedges
- A drizzle of olive oil
- 2 pounds of scored pork belly
- Salt and black pepper, as desired

Step-by-Step Directions to Cook It:

1. To a food processor, add the apples, sugar, and lemon juice. Pulse well to obtain a smooth mixture.
2. Coat the pork with the smooth mixture and set the rest aside.
3. Transfer the seasoned pork to the air fryer basket, position the broil, dehydration tray, and cover with the Instant Pot Duo Nova Air Fryer Lid.
4. Select the Roast Smart Program and set the timer for 40 minutes at 400°F.
5. Remove the lamb after roasting and set aside.
6. Pour the reserved apple mix into the inner pot of the air fryer and cover with the Instant Pot Duo Nova Air Fryer Lid. Select the Broil Smart Program and set the timer for 15 minutes at 300°F
7. Carve the lamb and serve with the sauce drizzled over the top.

Nutritional value per serving:

Calories: 456kcal, Fat: 34g, Carbs: 10g, Protein: 25g

Lemon Glazed Lamb

Glazing the lamb with lemon infuses it with a rich flavor that can be tasted when eating the lamb. This recipe will leave you eager for more.

Prep time and cooking time: 40 minutes | Serves: 4

Ingredients To Use:

- 2 lamb shanks
- Salt and black pepper, as desired
- 2 garlic cloves, minced
- 4 Tbsp. olive oil
- Juice from 1/2 lemon
- Zest from 1/2 lemon
- 1/2 tsp. oregano, dried

Step-by-Step Directions to Cook It:

1. Rub the lamb with garlic and season with salt and black pepper. Transfer to the air fryer basket of the instant Pot Air fryer.
2. Secure the Instant Pot Duo Nova Air Fryer Lid, select the Roast Smart Program, and set the timer for 40 minutes at 400°F.
3. While the lamb is roasting, mix the rest of the ingredients to make the lemon dressing. Add salt and black pepper to improve the taste.
4. Every 10 minutes, coat the lamb with the lemon dressing using a brush. Exercise caution while removing the Instant Pot Duo Nova Air Fryer Lid. Shred the lamb and serve.

Nutritional value per serving:

Calories: 260kcal, Fat: 7g, Carbs: 15g, Protein: 12g

Creamy Ham and Cauliflower

The 1 hour used for cooking in this recipe is to allow the ham to fully absorb the essence of the chicken stock and cauliflower juice. The result is fantastic.

Prep time and cooking time: 1 hour 10 minutes | Serves: 6

Ingredients To Use:

- 8 ounces of grated cheddar cheese
- 14 ounces of chicken stock
- 4 cup of cubed ham
- 1/2 tsp. garlic powder
- 4 garlic cloves, grated
- 1/2 tsp. onion powder
- Salt and black pepper, as desired
- 1/4 cup of heavy cream
- 16 ounces of cauliflower florets

Step-by-Step Directions to Cook It:

1. To a springform pan that fits your Instant Pot Air fryer, add the ham, chicken stock, cauliflower, and cheddar cheese.
2. Add the onion powder, garlic powder, garlic, salt, heavy cream, and black pepper. Stir and transfer to the Air Fryer.
3. Add the broil/dehydration tray, cover with the Instant Pot Duo Nova Air Fryer Lid, and select the Broil Smart program.
4. Set the timer for 1 hour at 300°F.
5. Press Start to begin cooking.
6. Divide into equal portions and serve.

Nutritional value per serving:

Calories: 320kcal, Fat: 20g, Carbs: 16g, Protein: 23g

Instant Air Fried Sausage and Mushrooms

The sausages and the mushroom slices are air-fried until they are crunchy and tasty. The fact that only a tsp of oil is used for frying is a marvel that is best performed with the Instant Pot Duo Nova Air Fryer Lid.

Prep time and cooking time: 50 minutes | Serves: 6

Ingredients To Use:

- 3 red bell peppers, sliced
- 1 Tbsp. brown sugar
- 2 pounds of sliced pork sausage
- 2 pounds of sliced Portobello mushrooms
- 2 sweet onions, chopped
- Salt and black pepper, as desired
- 1 tsp. olive oil

Step-by-Step Directions to Cook It:

1. In an oven-safe baking dish, mix the sausages with salt, black pepper, oil, mushrooms, bell pepper, sugar, and onions. Toss until the sausages and mushrooms are well-coated.
2. Transfer the coated mixture to the Instant Pot Air fryer and cover with the Instant Pot Duo Nova Air Fryer Lid.
3. Select the Air Fry Smart Program and set the timer for 40 minutes at 300°F.
4. Serve immediately.

Nutritional value per serving:

Calories: 130kcal, Fat: 12g, Carbs: 13g, Protein: 18g

Sausage and Kale Soup

Healthy and delicious. It can only get better when cooking with the Instant Pot Duo Nova Air Fryer Lid

Prep time and cooking time: 30 minutes | Serves: 4

Ingredients To Use:

- 1 cup of yellow onion, chopped
- 1 cup of water
- 1-1/2 pound of sliced Italian pork sausage
- 1/2 cup of chopped red bell pepper
- 5 pounds of chopped kale
- 1 tsp. garlic, grated
- Salt and black pepper, as desired
- 1/4 cup of chopped red hot chili pepper

Step-by-Step Directions to Cook It:

1. In a springform pan that fits the Instant Pot Air Fryer, mix the sausage slices, salt, pepper, onion, bell pepper, garlic, kale, chili pepper, and water.
2. Transfer the pan to the air fryer, cover with the Instant Pot Duo Nova Air Fryer Lid, and select the Broil Smart Program.
3. Adjust the time to 20 minutes and the temperature to 300°F
4. Divide into equal portions and serve.

Nutritional value per serving:

Calories: 150kcal, Fat: 4g, Carbs: 12g, Protein: 14g

Sirloin Steaks and Pico De Gallo

Experience a burst of flavor with this spice-rich recipe. The steaks are first seasoned with the first set of spices, then combined with the second set of spices after cooking.

Prep time and cooking time:20 minutes | Serves: 4

Ingredients To Use:

- 2 Tbsp. chili powder
- 1 tsp. garlic powder
- 4 medium sirloin steaks
- 1 tsp. cumin, ground
- 1 tsp. onion powder
- 1/2 Tbsp. sweet paprika
- Salt and black pepper, as desired
- Lemon wedges for garnish.

Pico de Gallo Ingredients:

- 1 small red onion, chopped
- 1/4 cup of chopped cilantro
- 2 tomatoes, chopped
- 2 garlic cloves, grated
- 1 small green bell pepper, chopped
- 1 jalapeno, chopped
- 2 Tbsp. lime juice
- 1/4 tsp. of ground cumin

Step-by-Step Directions to Cook It:

1. Mix the chili powder, black pepper, salt, garlic powder, onion powder, 1 tsp. cumin, and paprika in a small bowl. This will serve as the rub.
2. Season the steaks with the rub and transfer them to the air

fryer basket. Add the broil/dehydration tray and cover with the Instant Pot Duo Nova Air Fryer Lid.
3. Select the Roast Smart Program and set the timer for 10 minutes at 360°F.
4. In a separate bowl, mix the Pico de Gallo Ingredients until they are well combined.
5. Serve the steaks with the Pico de Gallo mix after cooking. Garnish with lemon wedges

Nutritional value per serving:

Calories: 200kcal, Fat: 12g, Carbs: 15g, Protein: 18g

Coffee Flavored Steaks

You don't have to rely on only espressos for your dose of coffee; you can also get it from your meals with this coffee glazed rib eye steaks.

Prep time and cooking time: 25 minutes | Serves: 4

Ingredients To Use:

- 1-1/2 Tbsp. of ground coffee
- A pinch of cayenne pepper
- 4 rib-eye steaks
- 1/4 tsp. of ground coriander
- 1/2 Tbsp. sweet paprika
- 2 tsp. garlic powder
- 2 Tbsp. chili powder
- 2 tsp. onion powder
- 1/4 tsp. ginger, ground
- Black pepper, as desired

Step-by-Step Directions to Cook It:

1. Mix the ground coffee, paprika, garlic, chili powder, coriander, onion powder, cayenne, garlic powder, and black pepper in a small bowl. This will serve as the rub.
2. Season the steaks with the rub, transfer it to the air fryer basket, and cover it with the Instant Pot Duo Nova Air Fryer Lid.
3. Select the Roast Smart Program and set the timer for 15 minutes at 360°F.
4. Divide the steaks into equal portions and serve with salad

Nutritional value per serving:

Calories: 160kcal, Fat: 10g, Carbs: 14g, Protein: 12g

Beef Kabobs

The skewers are first coated with an excellent combination of spices and then roasted until they are tasty and delicious.

Prep time and cooking time: 20 minutes | Serves: 4

Ingredients To Use:

- 2 red bell peppers, chopped
- 1/4 cup of salsa
- 2 pounds of chopped sirloin steak
- 1 red onion, chopped
- Juice from 1 lime
- 2 Tbsp. chili powder
- 1 zucchini, sliced
- 2 Tbsp. of hot sauce
- 1/2 Tbsp. of ground cumin
- 1/4 cup of olive oil
- Salt and black pepper, as desired

Step-by-Step Directions to Cook It:

1. Mix the salsa, hot sauce, lime juice, chili powder, salt, cumin, and black pepper in a small bowl.
2. Arrange the meat, zucchini, onions, and bell pepper on a skewer. Repeat the process until the ingredients are exhausted.
3. Coat the kabobs with the rub prepared earlier, transfer to the air fryer, and cover with the Instant Pot Duo Nova Air Fryer Lid.
4. Select the Roast Smart Program and set the timer for 10 minutes at 370°F.
5. Flip the skewers after 5 minutes.
6. Serve immediately with salad.

Nutritional value per serving:

Calories: 170kcal, Fat: 5g, Carbs: 13g, Protein: 16g

Chapter 6: Poultry Recipes

Honey Duck Breasts

The first coating is for the overall taste of the duck breast, while the second coating is to ensure that the deliciousness sticks to the duck's skin. Every bite of this meal tastes amazing.

Prep time and cooking time: 32 minutes | Serves: 2

Ingredients To Use:

- 1 smoked duck breast, halved
- 1 tsp. of honey
- 1 tsp. of tomato paste
- 1 Tbsp. of mustard
- 1/2 tsp. apple vinegar

Step-by-Step Directions to Cook It:

1. Mix the tomato paste, honey, mustard, vinegar, and duck breasts in a bowl.
2. Transfer the coated duck to the air fryer, cover with the Instant Pot Duo Nova Air Fryer Lid, and select the Air Fry Smart Program. Set the timer for 15 minutes at 370°F.
3. Remove the duck and recoat with the honey mix, then return to the air fryer for another round of cooking. Set the timer for 6 minutes.
4. Divide into equal portions and serve.

Nutritional value per serving:

Calories: 274kcal, Fat: 11g, Carbs: 22g, Protein: 13g

Chicken and Parsley Sauce

You are missing a lot if you've never tried coating chicken with red wine before roasting or grilling. The taste is out of this world. Try it now with the Instant Pot Duo Nova Air Fryer Lid, and you won't regret it.

Prep time and cooking time: 55 minutes | Serves: 6

Ingredients To Use:

- 1 cup of chopped parsley
- 12 chicken drumsticks
- 1 tsp. of dried oregano
- 1/2 cup of olive oil
- 4 garlic cloves
- 2 carrots, chopped
- A pinch of salt
- 1/4 cup of red wine
- A drizzle of maple syrup

Step-by-Step Directions to Cook It:

1. To a food processor, add the wine, oregano, parsley, salt, oil, garlic, and maple syrup. Pulse until a smooth mixture is obtained.
2. Add the chicken to the red wine mix and keep in the refrigerator for 30 minutes.
3. Remove chicken from the mixture and transfer to the air fryer basket. Reserve the red wine mix.
4. Cover the Instant Pot cooker base with the Instant Pot Duo Nova Air Fryer Lid and select the Roast Smart Program and set the timer for 25 minutes at 380°F.
5. Turn the food when the appliance brings up the notification.

6. Serve with reserved parsley sauce. Garnish with chopped carrots

Nutritional value per serving:

Calories: 354kcal, Fat: 10g, Carbs: 22g, Protein: 17g

Chicken and Green Onions Sauce

The green onions add a unique aroma and taste to the chicken. Try this recipe out to discover the real meaning of delicious.

Prep time and cooking time: 26 minutes | Serves: 4

Ingredients To Use:

- 10 green onions, coarsely chopped
- 1 Tbsp. lime juice
- inch piece ginger root, chopped
- 1/4 cup of chopped cilantro
- 4 garlic cloves, grated
- 1 tsp. butter, melted
- 2 Tbsp. fish sauce
- 3 Tbsp. soy sauce
- 1 tsp. Chinese five-spice
- 1 cup of coconut milk
- 10 chicken breasts
- Salt and black pepper, as desired

Step-by-Step Directions to Cook It:

1. Add the green onion, ginger, soy sauce, garlic, fish sauce, salt, five-spice, black pepper, coconut milk, and butter to a food processor and pulse until smooth.
2. Coat the chicken with the coconut milk mix, transfer to an oven-safe baking dish, and place it in the Instant Pot air fryer. Cover with the Instant Pot Duo Nova Air Fryer Lid and select the Broil Smart Program and set the timer for 16 minutes at 370°F.
3. Shake the fryer after 10 minutes of cooking.
4. Serve hot.

Nutritional value per serving:

Calories: 321kcal, Fat: 12g, Carbs: 22g, Protein: 20g

Baked Greek Chicken

Baking is another method that allows you to cook chicken without consuming a lot of oil. Here, the trace amount of olive oil is used to make the ingredients stick to the skin of the chicken breasts.

Prep time and cooking time: 25 minutes | Serves: 4

Ingredients To Use:

- 2 Tbsp. olive oil
- Juice from 1 lemon
- 1 tsp. of dried oregano
- 3 garlic cloves, grated
- 1 pound of chicken breasts
- Salt and black pepper, as desired
- 1/2 pound ofof trimmed asparagus
- 1 zucchini, roughly chopped
- 1 lemon sliced

Step-by-Step Directions to Cook It:

1. In an oven-safe baking dish, mix the breasts, oil, oregano, lemon juice, asparagus, garlic, oregano, salt, lemon slice, zucchini, and black pepper. Stir until chicken is well-coated.
2. Transfer the baking dish to the Instant Pot air fryer and cover with the Instant Pot Duo Nova Air Fryer Lid.
3. Select the Bake Smart Program and set the timer for 15 minutes at 380°F.
4. Divide into plates and serve.

Nutritional value per serving:

Calories: 300kcal, Fat: 8g, Carbs: 20g, Protein: 18g

Cider-Glazed Chicken

The chicken is briefly infused with flavor during the initial sautéing and then allowed to marinate for a few minutes before cooking with the rest of the ingredients.

Prep time and cooking time: 24 minutes | Serves: 4

Ingredients To Use:

- 1 sweet potato, cubed
- 1 Tbsp. mustard
- 2 apples, cored and sliced
- 1 Tbsp. butter
- 1 Tbsp. olive oil
- 1 Tbsp. rosemary, chopped
- 6 chicken thighs, bone-in and skin-on
- 2/3 cup of apple cider
- Salt and black pepper, as desired
- 1 Tbsp. butter
- 2 Tbsp. honey

Step-by-Step Directions to Cook It:

1. Using the Instant Pot cooker base, select Sauté, and heat the oil. Add the honey, cider, butter, and mustard. Stir and bring to a simmer. Add the chicken for a brief moment to coat, then remove from heat and set aside.
2. Mix the apples, rosemary, oil, salt, and black pepper in a medium bowl. Add to the reserved chicken.
3. Transfer the coated chicken and mixture to the inner pot of the air fryer and cover with the Instant Pot Duo Nova Air Fryer Lid.
4. Select the Broil Smart Program and adjust the time to 14 minutes and the temperature to 390°F
5. Divide into plates and serve.

Nutritional value per serving:

Calories: 241kcal, Fat: 7g, Carbs: 28g, Protein: 22g

Turkey, Peas, and Mushroom Casserole

The turkey and chicken stock adds pizzazz to this delicious mushroom casserole.

Prep time and cooking time: 30 minutes | Serves: 4

Ingredients To Use:

- 1 cup of bread cubes
- 2 pounds of turkey breasts, skinned and deboned
- 1 yellow onion, sliced
- 1/2 cup of peas
- 1 celery stalk, sliced
- 1 cup of chicken stock
- 1 cup of cream mushrooms soup
- Salt and black pepper, as desired

Step-by-Step Directions to Cook It:

1. In a springform pan, mix the turkey, salt, onion, pepper, celery, stock, and peas.
2. Transfer the pan to the Instant Pot cooker base, add the broil/dehydration tray, and cover with the Instant Pot Duo Nova Air Fryer Lid.
3. Set the timer for 15 minutes at 360°F.
4. Open the Instant Pot Duo Nova Air Fryer Lid, add the cream of mushroom soup and bread cubes, and cover the air fryer again. Cook at the same temperature for 5 more minutes.
5. Divide into equal portions and serve immediately.

Nutritional value per serving:

Calories: 271kcal, Fat: 9g, Carbs: 16g, Protein: 7g

Chicken Tenders and Flavored Sauce

Do you like your chicken deliciously air fried and yummy?
Then this recipe is perfect for you.
Prep time and cooking time: 30 minutes | Serves: 6

Ingredients To Use:

- 1 tsp. chili powder
- 2 tsp. garlic powder
- 1 tsp. onion powder
- 1 tsp. sweet paprika
- Salt and black pepper, as desired
- 2 Tbsp. butter
- 2 Tbsp. olive oil
- 2 pounds of chicken tenders
- 2 Tbsp. cornstarch
- 1/2 cup of chicken stock
- 2 cups of heavy cream
- 2 Tbsp. water
- 2 Tbsp. parsley, chopped

Step-by-Step Directions to Cook It:

1. Mix the garlic powder, onion powder, salt, black pepper, chili, and paprika in a medium bowl. This will serve as the rub.
2. Coat the chicken tenders with the rub, drizzle with oil, and place in the Instant Pot cooker base.
3. Cover with the Instant Pot Duo Nova Air Fryer Lid and select the Air Fry Smart Program. Set the timer for 10 minutes at 360°F.
4. After air frying, set the chicken aside.
5. Set the empty cooker base to Sauté mode and melt the butter. Stir in the chicken stock, cornstarch, cream, parsley, and water. Cover with the Instant Pot Duo Nova Air Fryer Lid and set to the Broil Smart Program for 10 minutes at 360°F. Serve the chicken and drizzle with the sauce.

Nutritional value per serving:

Calories: 351kcal, Fat: 12g, Carbs: 20g, Protein: 17g

Chicken and Radish Mix

Experience finger-licking goodness with this fantastic chicken and vegetable meal.

Prep time and cooking time: 40 minutes | Serves: 4

Ingredients To Use:

- 4 chicken things, bone-in
- Salt and black pepper, as desired
- 1 Tbsp. olive oil
- 1 cup of chicken stock
- 6 radishes, halved
- 1 tsp. sugar
- 3 carrots, cut into thin rounds
- 2 Tbsp. chives, chopped

Step-by-Step Directions to Cook It:

1. Set the empty cooker base to Sauté mode and heat the stock. Stir carrots, radishes, and sugar. Cover with the Instant Pot Duo Nova Air Fryer Lid and set to the Broil Smart Program for 20 minutes at 360°F. Set the sauce aside.
2. Season the chicken with salt and black pepper, then rub with oil.
3. Transfer the chicken to air fryer basket, cover with the Instant Pot Duo Nova Air Fryer Lid, and set to the Air Fry Smart Program.
4. Set the timer for 4 minutes at 350°F—select Start to begin.
5. When the chicken is done, add the radish sauce to the Instant Pot cooker base and cook for another 4 minutes.
6. Divide into equal portions and serve immediately.

Nutritional value per serving:

Calories: 237kcal, Fat: 10g, Carbs: 19g, Protein: 29g

Chicken Breast with Passion Fruit Sauce

The passion fruit adds a tropical flavor to the chicken. The fragrance also combines well with the aroma of the chicken.

Prep time and cooking time: 20 minutes | Serves: 4

Ingredients To Use:

- 4 chicken breasts
- Salt and black pepper, as desired
- 4 passion fruits, halved, deseeded and pulp reserved
- 1 Tbsp. whiskey
- 2-star anises
- 2 ounces maple syrup
- 1 bunch chives, chopped

Step-by-Step Directions to Cook It:

1. Set the empty cooker base to Sauté mode and heat the passion fruit pulp. Stir in the whiskey, maple syrup, star anise, and chives. Cover with the Instant Pot Duo Nova Air Fryer Lid and set to the Broil Smart Program for 6 minutes at 360°F. Set aside.
2. Rub the chicken with salt and black pepper, then transfer to the air fryer basket, cover with the Instant Pot Duo Nova Air Fryer Lid.
3. Select the Air Fry Smart Program.
4. Divide the chicken into equal portions and drizzle with the chicken sauce.
5. Serve.

Nutritional value per serving:

Calories: 374kcal, Fat: 8g, Carbs: 34g, Protein: 37g

Duck and Plum Sauce

The duck is cooked with the plum sauce to improve the rate of absorption. Every bite of this lovely delicacy drips with deliciousness.

Prep time and cooking time: 40 minutes | Serves: 2

Ingredients To Use:

- 2 duck breasts
- 1 Tbsp. butter, melted
- star anise
- 1 Tbsp. olive oil
- 1 shallot, chopped
- 9 ounces red plumps, stoned, cut into small wedges
- 2 Tbsp. sugar
- 2 Tbsp. red wine
- 1 cup of beef stock

Step-by-Step Directions to Cook It:

1. Set the empty cooker base to Sauté mode and heat the oil. Stir in the shallot and fry for 5 minutes.
2. Add the plums and sugar. Heat until the sugar dissolves.
3. Add the wine and stock, cook for another 15 minutes, then transfer the contents to a bowl. Set aside.
4. Season the duck with salt and black pepper, rub with the melted butter, then transfer to an oven-safe baking dish that fits the Instant Pot cooker base.
5. Add the star anise and plum sauce, then cover with the Instant Pot Duo Nova Air Fryer Lid. Set the Air Fry Smart Program for 12 minutes at 360°F.
6. Divide into equal portions and serve immediately.

Nutritional value per serving:

Calories: 400kcal, Fat: 25g, Carbs: 29g, Protein: 44g

Chapter 7: Seafood Recipes

Instant Air Fried Branzino

With the Instant Pot Duo Nova Air Fryer Lid, this recipe results in crispy, crunchy delicious branzino fillets.

Prep time and cooking time: 20 minutes | Serves: 4

Ingredients To Use:

- 1 lemon, zested and grated
- A pinch of red pepper flakes, crushed
- 1 orange, zested and grated
- 1/2 lemon, juiced
- 1/2 orange, juiced
- 4 medium branzino fillets, boneless
- 1/2 cup of parsley, chopped
- 2 Tbsp. olive oil
- Salt and black pepper, as desired

Step-by-Step Directions to Cook It:

1. Mix the fish fillets, orange and lemon zest, lemon and orange juice, salt, black pepper, pepper flakes, and oil in a large bowl.
2. Transfer the coated fillets to the air fryer basket and cover with the Instant Pot Duo Nova Air Fryer Lid. Select the Air Fry Smart program and set the timer for 10 minutes at 350°F.
3. Turn the food when directed to by the Lid.
4. Divide the fish into equal portions and serve immediately.

Nutritional value per serving:

Calories: 261kcal, Fat: 8g, Carbs: 21g, Protein: 12g

Marinated Salmon

This salmon is infused with taste during the 1 hour that it is kept in the fridge. Air frying the marinated salmon will result in a crispy and tasty meal.

Prep time and cooking time: 1 hour 20 minutes | Serves: 6

Ingredients To Use:

- 1 whole salmon
- 1 Tbsp. dill, chopped
- 1 Tbsp. tarragon, chopped
- 1 Tbsp. garlic, minced
- 2 lemons, juiced
- 1 lemon, sliced
- A pinch of salt and black pepper

Step-by-Step Directions to Cook It:

1. Season the fish with the salt, black pepper, and lemon juice. Keep in the refrigerator for 1 hour to marinate.
2. Stuff the salmon with the lemon and garlic slices, transfer to the air fryer basket, and cover with the Instant Pot Duo Nova Air Fryer Lid. Select the Air Fry Smart Program and cook for 25 minutes at 320°F.
3. Divide into equal portions and serve immediately. Serve with coleslaw.

Nutritional value per serving:

Calories: 300kcal, Fat: 8g, Carbs: 19g, Protein: 27g

Hawaiian Salmon

Are you in the mood for a well-seasoned, crunchy, and crispy fish meal? Then this is the perfect recipe for you.

Prep time and cooking time: 20 minutes | Serves: 2

Ingredients To Use:

- 20 ounces of canned pineapple pieces and juice
- 1/2 tsp. ginger, grated
- 2 tsp. garlic powder
- 1 tsp. onion powder
- 1 Tbsp. balsamic vinegar
- 2 medium salmon fillets, boneless
- Salt and black pepper, as desired

Step-by-Step Directions to Cook It:

1. Season the salmon with the garlic, onion, salt, and pepper.
2. Transfer the seasoned salmon to an oven-safe baking dish that fits into the Instant Pot cooker base.
3. Drizzle the salmon with vinegar and cover with the Instant Pot Duo Nova Air Fryer Lid. Select the Air Fry Smart Program and set the timer for 10 minutes at 350°F.
4. Divide into equal portions and serve immediately.

Nutritional value per serving:

Calories: 200kcal, Fat: 8g, Carbs: 17g, Protein: 20g

Chinese Cod

This recipe is perfect for lovers of Chinese flavor. The cod is adequately seasoned with ginger and soy sauce.

Prep time and cooking time: 20 minutes | Serves: 2

Ingredients To Use:

- 1 2 medium cod fillets, boneless
- 1 tsp. peanuts, crushed
- 2 tsp. garlic powder
- 1 Tbsp. light soy sauce
- 1/2 tsp. ginger, grated

Step-by-Step Directions to Cook It:

1. Place the cod fillets in the oven-safe baking dish and season with garlic, soy sauce, and ginger.
2. Transfer to the Instant Pot cooker base and cover with the Instant Pot Duo Nova Air Fryer Lid and select the Air Fry Smart Program.
3. Set the timer for 10 minutes at 350°F.
4. Divide into equal portions and sprinkle with peanuts.

Nutritional value per serving:

Calories: 254kcal, Fat: 10g, Carbs: 14g, Protein: 23g

Halibut and Sun-Dried Tomatoes Mix

The Halibut is coated with sun-dried tomatoes and air fried for delicious, crunchy goodness.

Prep time and cooking time: 20 minutes | Serves: 2

Ingredients To Use:

- 2 medium halibut fillets
- 2 garlic cloves, minced
- 2 tsp. olive oil
- Salt and black pepper, as desired
- 6 sun-dried tomatoes, chopped
- 2 small red onions, sliced
- 1 fennel bulb, sliced
- 9 black olives, pitted and sliced
- 4 rosemary springs, chopped
- 1/2 tsp. red pepper flakes, crushed

Step-by-Step Directions to Cook It:

1. Coat the halibut fillets with the salt, pepper, garlic, and oil. Transfer to an oven-safe baking dish that fits into the Instant Pot cooker base.
2. Add the onion slices, tomatoes, olives, fennel, pepper flakes, and rosemary.
3. Transfer the dish to the air fryer, add the dehydration tray, and cover with the Instant Pot Duo Nova Air Fryer Lid.
4. Select the Air Fry Smart Program and set the timer for 10 minutes at 380°F.
5. Divide the fish and vegetables among plates and serve.

Nutritional value per serving:

Calories: 213kcal, Fat: 12g, Carbs: 23g, Protein: 17g

Stuffed Calamari

Whether fresh, frozen, large, or small calamari, this recipe works for all. Enjoy this lovely recipe with the Instant Pot Duo Nova Air Fryer Lid.

Prep time and cooking time: 35 minutes | Serves: 4

Ingredients To Use:

- 4 big calamari, tentacles separated and chopped and tubes reserved
- 2 Tbsp. parsley, chopped
- 5 ounces kale, chopped
- 2 garlic cloves, minced
- 1 red bell pepper, chopped
- 1 Tbsp. olive oil
- 2 ounces canned tomato puree
- 1 yellow onion, chopped
- Salt and black pepper, as desired

Step-by-Step Directions to Cook It:

1. Set the empty cooker base to Sauté mode and heat the oil. Stir in the garlic and onion—Fry for about 2 minutes.
2. Add the bell peppers, calamari tentacles, salt, pepper, tomato puree, and kale. Stir and cook for 10 minutes.
3. Transfer the contents of the air fryer to a bowl.
4. Stuff the calamari with the tomato puree mixture and hold with toothpicks.
5. Transfer the calamari to the air fryer, cover with the Instant Pot Duo Nova Air Fryer Lid, and select the Air Fry Smart Program.
6. Set the timer for 20 minutes at 360°F.
7. Divide into equal portions and sprinkle with parsley. Serve.

Nutritional value per serving:

Calories: 322kcal, Fat: 10g, Carbs: 14g, Protein: 22g

Crusted Salmon

You can get cooked salmons everywhere, at the store, restaurant, or even in your own home. With the Instant Pot Duo Nova Air Fryer Lid, you can make restaurant-worthy crusty salmon in your kitchen.

Prep time and cooking time: 20 minutes | Serves: 4

Ingredients To Use:

- 1 cup of pistachios, chopped
- 4 salmon fillets
- 1/4 cup of lemon juice
- 2 Tbsp. honey
- 1 tsp. dill, chopped
- Salt and black pepper, as desired
- 1 Tbsp. mustard

Step-by-Step Directions to Cook It:

1. Mix the pistachios, honey, mustard, dill, salt, black pepper, and lemon juice in a bowl. This will serve as the rub.
2. Coat the salmon with the rub and transfer to the air fryer basket.
3. Cover the Instant Pot cooker base with Instant Pot Air Fryer Lid and set the Air Fry Smart Program.
4. Set the timer for 10 minutes at 350°F
5. Divide into equal portions and serve with salad.

Nutritional value per serving:

Calories: 300kcal, Fat: 17g, Carbs: 20g, Protein: 22g

Swordfish and Mango Salsa

The mango sauce adds a delicious fruitiness to the Instant Roasted Swordfish steaks. Ensure you eat each bite with the mango salsa.

Prep time and cooking time: 16 minutes | Serves: 2

Ingredients To Use:

- 2 medium swordfish steaks
- Salt and black pepper, as desired
- 2 tsp. avocado oil
- 1 Tbsp. cilantro, chopped
- 1 mango, chopped
- 1 avocado, pitted, peeled and chopped
- A pinch of cumin
- A pinch of onion powder
- A pinch of garlic powder
- 1 orange, peeled and sliced
- 1/2 Tbsp. balsamic vinegar

Step-by-Step Directions to Cook It:

1. Rub the swordfish with onion, garlic, pepper, salt, cumin, and black pepper.
2. Rub the seasoned steaks with 1/2 the oil and transfer to the Air Fryer basket.
3. Cover with the Instant Pot cooker base with the Instant Pot Duo Nova Air Fryer Lid. Select the Roast Smart Program and set the timer to 6 minutes at 360°F.
4. Turn the food when directed by the appliance.
5. In a small bowl, mix the mango, avocado, cilantro, salt, vinegar, black pepper, and leftover oil.
6. Divide the roasted fish into equal portions and serve with the mango salsa and orange slices.

Nutritional value per serving:

Calories: 200kcal, Fat: 7g, Carbs: 14g, Protein: 14g

Squid and Guacamole

The squid is air fried and crunchy and then eaten with the delicious guacamole salad.

Prep time and cooking time: 20 minutes | Serves: 4

Ingredients To Use:

- 2 medium squids, tentacles separated and tubes scored lengthwise
- 1 Tbsp. olive oil
- Juice from 1 lime
- Salt and black pepper, as desired

Guacamole Ingredients:

- 2 avocados, pitted, peeled and chopped
- 1 Tbsp. coriander, chopped
- 2 red chilies, chopped
- 1 tomato, chopped
- 1 red onion, chopped
- 2 limes, juiced

Step-by-Step Directions to Cook It:

1. Season the squid and its tentacles with the salt, black pepper, and drizzle with olive oil.
2. Transfer the seasoned squid to the air fryer basket and cover with the Instant Pot Duo Nova Air Fryer Lid.
3. Select the Air Fry smart program and set the timer to 6 minutes and 360°F.
4. Remove the squid from the air fryer and drizzle with lime juice.

5. In a small bowl, mix the avocado, coriander, tomato, chilies, onion, and juice. Mash the ingredients together with a fork and stir well.
6. Serve the squids into plates and top with the guacamole.

Nutritional value per serving:

Calories: 260kcal, Fat: 7g, Carbs: 28g, Protein: 18g

Tuna and Chimichurri Sauce

The chimichurri sauce adds flavor and aroma to the arugula—the combination of the arugula and Tuna results in a fantastic combination.

Prep time and cooking time: 18 minutes | Serves: 4

Ingredients To Use:

- 1/2 cup of cilantro, chopped
- 1/3 cup of olive oil+ 2 Tbsp.
- 1 small red onion, chopped
- 3 Tbsp. balsamic vinegar
- 2 Tbsp. parsley, chopped
- 2 Tbsp. basil, chopped
- 1 jalapeno pepper, chopped
- 1 pound of sushi tuna steak
- Salt and black pepper, as desired
- 1 tsp. red pepper flakes
- 1 tsp. thyme, chopped
- 3 garlic cloves, minced
- 2 avocados, pitted, peeled and sliced
- 6 ounces baby arugula

Step-by-Step Directions to Cook It:

1. Mix the jalapeno pepper, onion, vinegar, basil, cilantro, garlic, pepper flakes, parsley, thyme, salt, and black pepper in a small bowl. Set aside.
2. Season with the tuna with salt, pepper, and oil.
3. Transfer the seasoned tuna to the air fryer and cover with the Instant Pot Duo Nova Air Fryer Lid.
4. Select the Bake Smart Program, and set the timer for 6 minutes at 360°F. Turn the food after 3 minutes.

5. Meanwhile, mix the arugula with 1/2 of the chimichurri mix prepared at the beginning. Toss vigorously to coat.
6. When ready, slice up the salmon.
7. Divide the arugula into two equal portions, add the sliced salmon, and top with the remnant of the chimichurri sauce.
8. Serve.

Nutritional value per serving:

Calories: 276kcal, Fat: 3g, Carbs: 14g, Protein: 20g

Chapter 8: Soups, Stews, and Broths

Creamy Chicken Stew

This stew is all shades of amazing. It is healthy, creamy, and delicious. You can eat this stew alone or as a side dish.

Prep time and cooking time: 35 minutes | Serves: 4

Ingredients To Use:

- 1-1/2 cup of canned cream of celery soup
- 6 chicken tenders
- Salt and black pepper, as desired
- 2 potatoes, chopped
- 1 bay leaf
- 1 thyme spring, chopped
- 1 Tbsp. milk
- 1 egg yolk
- 1/2 cup of heavy cream

Step-by-Step Directions to Cook It:

1. Mix the chicken, potatoes, cream of celery, thyme, bay leaf, salt, and black pepper. Toss until the chicken is well coated, then transfer to the basket of the air fryer.
2. Cover the air fryer with the Instant Pot Duo Nova Air Fryer Lid and select the Air Fry Smart Program.
3. Set the timer to 25 minutes and 320°F.

4. Allow the stew to cool for a few minutes, then discard the bay leaf and serve into plates.

Nutritional value per serving:

Calories: 300kcal, Fat: 11g, Carbs: 23g, Protein: 14g

Chicken Consommé

The egg white and eggshells used in this recipe is to make the soup sparkling clear. This is a shortcut recipe for a delicious meal.

Prep time and cooking time: 50 minutes | Serves: 4

Ingredients To Use:

- 6 cup of canned chicken broth
- 3 large egg, whites separated and whisked, shells reserved
- 3 scallions with tops, sliced
- 1 tomato, sliced
- 1 small carrot, sliced
- 1/2 cup of chopped fresh parsley
- 1/2 tsp. of dried thyme
- 1/2 tsp. of dried basil
- 6 whole black peppercorns
- 1 bay leaf

Step-by-Step Directions to Cook It:

1. Mix the broth, egg whites, shells, scallions, carrot, tomato, parsley, basil, thyme, bay leaf, and peppercorns. Transfer the mixture to the Instant Pot cooker base and cover with the Instant Pot Duo Nova Air Fryer Lid.
2. Select the Broil Smart Program and set the timer to 36 minutes at 370°F.
3. Sieve the soup through a fine-mesh into a heatproof dish. Discard the solids accumulated in the mesh, skim off the fat on the soup and serve into bowls.

Nutritional value per serving:

Calories: 130kcal, Fat: 13g, Carbs: 18g, Protein: 9g

Tofu Vegetable Soup

This deliciously light soup is packed with vitamin C and protein. It can be prepared in less than 20 minutes.

Prep time and cooking time: 15 minutes | Serves: 4

Ingredients To Use:

- 1-1/2 cup of chicken stock
- 2 Tbsp. rice vinegar
- 6 scallions, sliced
- 2 Tbsp. ketchup
- 1 Tbsp. sesame oil
- 3/4 tsp. salt
- 1 pound of firm tofu, divided into 1-inch chunks
- 3 cup of shredded Napa cabbage
- 2 carrots, sliced
- 1/2 tsp. ground ginger

Step-by-Step Directions to Cook It:

1. To the Instant Pot cooker base, add the water, chicken stock, ketchup, vinegar, salt, oil, and ginger.
2. Stir and cover with the broil/dehydration tray and the Instant Pot Duo Nova Air Fryer Lid. Set the timer to 10 minutes at 360°F.
3. After 5 minutes, carefully remove the cover of the instant pot and add the tofu, carrots, cabbage, and scallions. Leave to cook for the rest of the cooking time.
4. Divide into equal portions and serve.

Nutritional value per serving:

Calories: 154kcal, Fat: 7g, Carbs: 9g, Protein: 14g

Greek Egg and Lemon Soup

This is a classic Greek soup that can serve as a first course for lunch and dinner.

Prep time and cooking time: 50 minutes | Serves: 6

Ingredients To Use:

- 1 Tbsp. olive oil
- 1 yellow onion, thinly sliced
- 6 lemon slices
- 8 cups of homemade chicken stock
- 2 eggs, whisked
- 1/3 cup of lemon juice
- 1-1/2 tsp. salt
- Snipped dill sprigs
- 1/4 cup of fresh dill

Step-by-Step Directions to Cook It:

1. Set the empty cooker base to Sauté mode and heat the oil. Stir in the oil and fry for 3 minutes.
2. Add the chicken stock, and cover with the Instant Pot Duo Nova Air Fryer Lid. Select the Broil Smart Program and set the timer to 20 minutes at 300°F.
3. After 20 minutes, add the eggs, lemon juice, and salt. Replace the Instant Pot Duo Nova Air Fryer Lid and select the Broil Smart Program at 250°F for 3 minutes.
4. Serve.

Nutritional value per serving:

Calories: 98kcal, Fat: 4g, Carbs: 8g, Protein: 2g

Chive Vichyssoise

Here is a chilled potato soup that is sure to improve the flavor of your entire meal. Buttermilk, rather than heavy cream, is used to reduce the calorie content.

Prep time and cooking time: 30 minutes | Serves: 4

Ingredients To Use:

- 1 Tbsp. unsalted butter
- 2 tsp. of lemon juice
- 1 medium yellow onion, sliced
- 1 medium leek, sliced
- 1/4 tsp. of hot red pepper sauce
- 1 medium celery stalk, sliced
- 2 medium potatoes, peeled and cubed
- 1 3/4 cup of chicken broth
- 1 cup of buttermilk
- 1 Tbsp. minced fresh chives

Step-by-Step Directions to Cook It:

1. Set the empty cooker base to Sauté mode and melt the butter. Stir in the onions, celery, and leek. Sauté for 3 minutes.
2. Add the broth, set the broil/dehydration tray, and cover with the Instant Pot Duo Nova Air Fryer Lid.
3. Set the timer to 20 minutes at 350°F.
4. Transfer the soup to a food processor and blend for 30 seconds. Add the chives, lemon juice, buttermilk, pepper sauce, and lemon juice.
5. Transfer the blended mixture to a bowl and keep in the refrigerator for 3 hours. Serve.

Nutritional value per serving:

Calories: 121kcal, Fat: 9g, Carbs: 15g, Protein: 8g

White Borscht

White Borscht is a popular European recipe that is cooked with potatoes rather than beets. It is delicious and easy.

Prep time and cooking time: 30 minutes | Serves: 4

Ingredients To Use:

- 3/4 pound of red potatoes, thinly sliced
- 3 cups of buttermilk
- 1 large cucumber, thinly sliced
- 1 small red onion, thinly sliced
- 1/3 cup of walnuts
- 3/4 tsp. salt
- 3 chicken sausages, sliced
- 1/2 tsp. black pepper
- 3/4 cup of thinly sliced radishes, cut thinly
- 1/4 cup of snipped fresh dill

Step-by-Step Directions to Cook It:

1. Add the potatoes to the Instant Pot cooker base, add water to cover, then seal with the Instant Pot Duo Nova Air Fryer Lid.
2. Select the Smart Broil program and set the timer for 10 minutes at 350°F.
3. Remove the cooked potatoes, drain, and set aside
4. Add the cucumber, walnuts, onion, salt, pepper, and 2 cups of buttermilk to a food processor and pulse until a smooth mixture is obtained.
5. Serve the walnut mixture into bowls, stir in the leftover buttermilk, reserved potatoes, dill, and radishes.
6. Cover the bowls and keep refrigerated for 3 hours.
7. Serve cold.

Nutritional value per serving:

Calories: 145kcal, Fat: 14g, Carbs: 19g, Protein: 8g

Chunky Seafood Chowder

This seafood chowder recipe is the complete package. It is rich with crab, soft potatoes, onions, and clams.

Prep time and cooking time: 35 minutes | Serves: 8

Ingredients To Use:

- 2 Tbsp. butter
- 1 medium onion, chopped
- 2 pints of half-and-half
- 1 can of New England clam chowder
- 3 medium potatoes, diced
- 1 tsp. salt
- 1/4 tsp. white pepper
- 8 ounces of crabmeat, flaked

Step-by-Step Directions to Cook It:

1. Set the empty cooker base to Sauté mode and melt the butter. Stir in the onion and fry for about 2 minutes.
2. Add the clam chowder, half and half, potatoes, salt, and black pepper. Cover with the broil/dehydration tray and the Instant Pot Duo Nova Air Fryer Lid.
3. Select the Broil Smart Program and set the timer for 15 minutes at 370°F.
4. When ready, add the crab meat and cook for another 8 minutes at the same temperature.

Nutritional value per serving:

Calories: 189kcal, Fat: 13g, Carbs: 23g, Protein: 11g

Gingered Tofu and Noodle Soup

The ginger and scallions used in this recipe add a spark to this otherwise delicate soup.

Prep time and cooking time: 30 minutes | Serves: 4

Ingredients To Use:

- 8 ounces of fine egg noodles, cooked
- 2 Tbsp. olive oil
- 5 scallions, sliced into 1-inch slices
- 3 Tbsp. minced fresh ginger
- 5 cups of chicken stock
- 1 small head cabbage, thinly sliced
- 12 ounces of firm tofu, chopped into 1/2-inch cubes
- 1/4 tsp. salt
- 1/8 tsp. of black pepper

Step-by-Step Directions to Cook It:

1. Toss the cooked noodles with 1 tbsp of olive oil.
2. Set the empty cooker base to Sauté mode and heat the oil. Stir in the ginger and scallions—Fry for about 2 minutes.
3. Add the stock and cabbage, then cover with the broil/dehydration tray and the Instant Pot Duo Nova Air Fryer Lid.
4. Select the Broil Smart Program and set the timer for 10 minutes at 350°F.
5. Stir in the tofu, noodles, and season with salt and black pepper.
6. Allow cooling for 2 minutes before serving.

Nutritional value per serving:

Calories: 136kcal, Fat: 12g, Carbs: 17g, Protein: 8g

Minestrone

The beauty of a Minestrone is that everything goes as long as it's a hearty mixture of vegetables, pasta, rice, or white beans. For vegetarians, the beef stock can be substituted with vegetable broth.

Prep time and cooking time: 50 minutes | Serves: 6

Ingredients To Use:

- 1 Tbsp. olive oil
- 1 large yellow onion, chopped
- 2 garlic cloves, grated
- 3-1/2 cup of beef broth
- 15 ounces of great Northern beans, rinsed and drained
- 1-3/4 cup of chopped tomatoes, cut up and left undrained
- 2 cups of roughly shredded cabbage
- 2 large carrots, thinly chopped
- 1 tsp. dried oregano
- 1 tsp. dried basil
- 1/2 tsp. salt
- 1/2 tsp. black pepper
- 2 ounces of vermicelli, broken
- 1 small zucchini, and sliced
- Shredded Parmesan cheese

Step-by-Step Directions to Cook It:

1. Set the empty cooker base to Sauté mode and heat the oil. Stir in the garlic and onion—Fry for about 3 minutes.
2. Add the broth, tomatoes, beans, cabbage, oregano, carrots, basil, salt, and black pepper.

3. Cover with the broil/dehydration tray and the Instant Pot Duo Nova Air Fryer Lid. Select the Broil Smart Program and set the timer for 5 minutes at 350°F.
4. Add the vermicelli and replace the cover.
5. Increase the timer of the Instant Pot Duo Nova Air Fryer Lid to 15 minutes. Maintain the same temperature.
6. Add the zucchini, cook for another 33 minutes, then transfer the contents to plates.
7. Serve with grated cheese.

Nutritional value per serving:

Calories: 259kcal, Fat: 26g, Carbs: 31g, Protein: 8g

Hot, Hot Chili Soup

This recipe is for the lovers of spicy soup. It is dangerously hot and spicy and is not for the meek. If you love a good spicy meal, challenge yourself with this recipe.

Prep time and cooking time: 2 hours 10 minutes | Serves: 8

Ingredients To Use:

- 2 Tbsp. vegetable oil
- 2 pounds of beef stew meat, cut into pieces
- 1 medium onion, thinly sliced
- 3 garlic cloves, grated
- 16 ounces of hot banana peppers, chopped
- 29 ounces of diced tomatoes, left undrained
- 10 ounces of diced tomatoes and green chiles, left undrained
- 6 ounces of tomato paste
- 16 ounces of kidney beans, rinsed and drained
- 4 ounces of chopped green chiles
- 1 fresh jalapeno pepper, seeded and chopped
- 2 Tbsp. chili powder
- 1-1/2 Tbsp. hot red pepper sauce
- 1 tsp. salt
- 1/8 tsp. ground cumin
- Whole banana peppers

Step-by-Step Directions to Cook It:

1. Set the empty cooker base to Sauté mode and heat the oil. Stir in the garlic, beef, and onion. Fry for about 5 minutes until meat is browned.

2. Add the chopped hot peppers, diced tomatoes, tomato paste, tomato and chiles, chili powder, jalapeno pepper, cumin, red pepper sauce, and sauce.
3. Cover with the broil/dehydration tray and the Instant Pot Duo Nova Air Fryer Lid. Select the Broil Smart Program and set the timer for 2 hours at 300°F.
4. Garnish with whole banana peppers and serve.

Nutritional value per serving:

Calories: 131kcal, Fat: 6g, Carbs: 12g, Protein: 8g

Chapter 9: Rice, Multi-grain, and Porridges

Rice, Almonds and Raisins Pudding

This recipe results in a delicacy fit for kings. The Instant Pot Duo Nova Air Fryer Lid is a premium rice cooker.

Prep time and cooking time: 15 minutes | Serves: 4

Ingredients To Use:

- 1 cup of brown rice
- 1/2 cup of coconut chips
- 1 cup of milk
- 2 cups of water
- 1/2 cup of maple syrup
- 1/4 cup of raisins
- 1/4 cup of almonds
- A pinch of cinnamon powder

Step-by-Step Directions to Cook It:

1. Add the rice to a springform pan that fits the Instant Pot cooker base, stir in the water and cover with the Instant Pot Duo Nova Air Fryer Lid.
2. Select the Broil Smart Program and set the timer for 15 minutes at 350°F.
3. Drain the rice, then add the raisins, almonds, maple syrup, cinnamon, and stir.

4. Replace the Instant Pot Duo Nova Air Fryer Lid and reset the time to 8 minutes at the same Smart Program and temperature.
5. Serve the rice puddings into bowls.

Nutritional value per serving:

Calories: 251kcal, Fat: 6g, Carbs: 39g, Protein: 12g

Rice and Sausage Side Dish

An exquisite side dish that will improve your appetite and leave you hungry for more.

Prep time and cooking time: 30 minutes | Serves: 4

Ingredients To Use:

- 2 cups of white rice, boiled
- 1 Tbsp. butter
- Salt and black pepper, as desired
- 4 garlic cloves, grated
- 1 pork sausage, sliced
- 2 Tbsp. carrot, chopped
- 3 Tbsp. cheddar cheese, shredded
- 2 Tbsp. mozzarella cheese, grated

Step-by-Step Directions to Cook It:

1. Set the empty cooker base to Sauté mode at 350°F and melt the butter. Stir in the garlic and brown for about 2 minutes.
2. Stir in the sausage, carrots, rice, pepper, and salt. Cover with the broil/dehydration tray and the Instant Pot Duo Nova Air Fryer Lid.
3. Select the Broil Smart Program and set the timer for 10 minutes at 350°F.
4. Top with the mozzarella and cheddar and serve.

Nutritional value per serving:

Calories: 240kcal, Fat: 12g, Carbs: 20g, Protein: 13g

Blueberry and Brown Sugar Oatmeal

This is an incredibly easy recipe that can serve as a breakfast or a quick snack. Try it now with the Instant Pot Duo Nova Air Fryer Lid.

Prep time and cooking time: 20 minutes | Serves: 4

Ingredients To Use:

- 1 cup of traditional rolled oats
- 1/2 tsp. cinnamon
- 1/2 tsp. of baking powder
- 1 medium egg
- 1/2 tsp. of nutmeg
- 1 cup of milk
- 3/4 cup of brown sugar
- Cooking spray

Step-by-Step Directions to Cook It:

1. Add the egg and milk to a bowl and whisk until well-combined.
2. Grease an oven-safe baking dish with the cooking spray and set aside.
3. In a separate bowl, mix the oats, cinnamon, brown sugar, nutmeg, and baking powder.
4. To the greased baking dish, add a quarter of the berries. This will serve as the bottom layer.
5. Add the entire egg mix. This will serve as the second layer.
6. Add the entire oat mix. This will serve as the third layer.
7. Cover the layers with the rest of the berries. Allow to rest for 10 minutes before transferring to the air fryer.
8. Cover with the Instant Pot Duo Nova Air Fryer Lid and select the Bake Smart Program. Set the timer to 10 minutes at 320°F. Slice and serve.

Nutritional value per serving:

Calories: 154kcal, Fat: 11g, Carbs: 15g, Protein: 8g

Wide Rice Pilaf

The wild rice is seasoned with spices, vegetables, and nuts, then transferred to the air fryer to boil and absorb the delectable taste of the chicken stock.

Prep time and cooking time: 35 minutes | Serves: 12

Ingredients To Use:

- 1 shallot, sliced
- 1 tsp. garlic, grated
- A drizzle of olive oil
- 1 cup of faro
- 3/4 cup of wild rice
- 4 cups of chicken stock
- Salt and black pepper, as desired
- 1 Tbsp. of chopped parsley
- 1/2 cup of toasted, chopped hazelnuts
- 3/4 cup of dried cherries
- Chopped chives, garnish

Step-by-Step Directions to Cook It:

1. In an oven-proof baking dish, mix the garlic, oil, shallots, faro, rice, salt, black pepper, parsley, cherries, stock, and hazelnuts.
2. Transfer the dish to the Instant Pot Air fryer basket and cover with the broil/dehydration tray and the Instant Pot Duo Nova Air Fryer Lid.
3. Select the Broil Smart Program and set the timer for 25 minutes at 350°F.
4. Divide into equal portions and serve.

Nutritional value per serving:

Calories: 142kcal, Fat: 4g, Carbs: 16g, Protein: 4g

Pumpkin Rice

This meal can serve as a side dish or a main meal when you are interested in having a light lunch.

Prep time and cooking time: 35 minutes | Serves: 4

Ingredients To Use:

- 2 Tbsp. olive oil
- 1 small yellow onion, sliced
- 2 garlic cloves, grated
- 12 ounces of white rice
- 4 cup of chicken stock
- 6 ounces of pumpkin puree
- 1/2 tsp. nutmeg
- 1 tsp. of chopped thyme
- 1/2 tsp. of grated ginger
- 1/2 tsp. cinnamon powder
- 1/2 tsp. of allspice
- 4 ounces of heavy cream

Step-by-Step Directions to Cook It:

1. In an oven-proof baking dish, mix the rice, stock, oil, onion, pumpkin puree, garlic, nutmeg, ginger, thyme, cinnamon, cream, and allspice.
2. Transfer the pan to the Instant pot's air fryer basket and cover with the broil/dehydration tray and the Instant Pot Duo Nova Air Fryer Lid.
3. Select the Broil Smart Program and set the timer for 30 minutes at 360°F.
4. Divide into equal portions and serve as a side dish.

Nutritional value per serving:

Calories: 261kcal, Fat: 6g, Carbs: 19g, Protein: 4g

Wild Rice Soup

A spoon of this soup contains wild rice and a combination of spices that will cause an explosion of flavor in your mouth.

Prep time and cooking time: 1 hour | Serves: 8

Ingredients To Use:

- 1/3 cup of uncooked wild rice
- 1 Tbsp. vegetable oil
- 1/2 cup of butter
- 1 medium onion, thinly sliced
- 1 celery stalk, chopped
- 1 carrot, finely chopped
- 1/2 cup of all-purpose flour
- 3 cups of chicken stock
- 2 cups of half-and-half
- 1/2 tsp. of dried rosemary
- 1 tsp. salt

Step-by-Step Directions to Cook It:

1. Wash the rice and drain it.
2. Add the rice, oil, and 1 quart of water to the Instant Pot cooker base and cover with the Instant Pot Duo Nova Air Fryer Lid.
3. Select the Broil Smart Program and set the timer for 30 minutes at 300°F.
4. After the rice is done, transfer the contents of the air fryer to a bowl.
5. Melt the butter in the now-empty cooker base, and sauté the celery, onion, and carrot until they are tender.
6. Stir in the flour and cook for another 3 minutes. Stir in the stock, rosemary, half and half, and boiled rice. Cover the

air fryer with the Instant Pot Duo Nova Air Fryer Lid and set the timer for 20 minutes at the same temperature and Smart program.

Nutritional value per serving:

Calories: 217kcal, Fat: 13g, Carbs: 17g, Protein: 10g

Rice Stuffed Bell Pepper Soup

Pamper your palates with this delicious treat. The bell peppers are stuffed with well-spiced and tasty rice.

Prep time and cooking time: | Serves: 16

Ingredients To Use:

- 1 pound of ground beef
- 4 cups of tomato juice
- 3 red or green bell peppers, cored, diced
- 1-1/2 cups of chili sauce
- 1 cup of long-grain rice
- 2 celery stalks, chopped
- 1 large onion, sliced
- 3 chicken bouillon cubes
- 2 garlic cloves, grated
- 1/2 tsp. salt
- 2 tsp. browning sauce
- Salt and black pepper, as desired

Step-by-Step Directions to Cook It:

1. Season the beef with the salt and black pepper before transferring to the air fryer basket and covering with the Instant Pot Duo Nova Air Fryer Lid.
2. Select the Air Fry Smart Program and use the default timer.
3. When the beef is ready, add the stock, peppers, tomato juice, celery, rice, onion, chili sauce, bouillon cubes, browning sauce, salt, and 8 cups of water.
4. Replace the Instant Pot Duo Nova Air Fryer Lid and select the Dehydrate Smart Program and set the timer for 1 hour at 300°F.
5. Divide into equal portions and serve.

Nutritional value per serving:

Calories: 157kcal, Fat: 8g, Carbs: 12g, Protein: 6g

Fresh Baked Oatmeal

Oatmeals always turn out great when prepared with the help of the Instant Pot Duo Nova Air Fryer Lid. Try out this meal to experience the fantastic taste.

Prep time and cooking time: 30 minutes | Serves: 4

Ingredients To Use:

- 1 cup of milk
- 1/6 cup of brown sugar
- 1 large egg
- 2 cups of strawberries, halved
- 1 cup of traditionally rolled oats
- 1/2 tsp. of ground cinnamon
- 1/3 tsp. of salt
- 1/2 tsp. of baking powder
- 1/8 cup of slivered almonds
- Cooking spray

Step-by-Step Directions to Cook It:

1. Add the egg and milk to a bowl and whisk until well-combined.
2. In a medium bowl, mix the oats, sugar, baking powder, salt, and cinnamon. Stir thoroughly until well-combined.
3. Grease an oven-safe baking dish with the cooking spray and set aside.
4. Arrange a quarter of the strawberries at the bottom of the dish, layer with the oats mix, then the egg mix, and finally top with the rest of the berries.
5. Allow to rest for 10 minutes, then sprinkle with nutmeg and almonds.

6. Transfer the dish to the Instant Pot cooker base, cover with the Instant Pot Duo Nova Air Fryer Lid and select the Bake Smart Program.
7. Set the timer for 10 minutes at 320°F.
8. Allow to cool, slice, and serve.

Nutritional value per serving:

Calories: 153kcal, Fat: 11g, Carbs: 9g, Protein: 7g

Chapter 10: Beans, Chilis, and Eggs

French Beans and Egg Breakfast Mix

The combination of beans and eggs is healthy and delicious. With the Instant Pot Duo Nova Air Fryer Lid, you can eat healthily and deliciously.

Prep time and cooking time: 30 minutes | Serves: 3

Ingredients To Use:

- 2 eggs, whisked
- 1/2 tsp. of soy sauce
- 1 Tbsp. olive oil
- 4 garlic cloves, minced
- 3 ounces of trimmed French beans
- Salt and white pepper, as desired

Step-by-Step Directions to Cook It:

1. Mix the eggs and soy sauce in a bowl. Season with salt and black pepper, then whisk thoroughly.
2. Set the empty cooker base to Sauté mode at 320°F and heat the oil. Stir in the garlic and brown for about 1 minute.
3. Add the egg mix and French beans to the cooker base, cover with the Instant Pot Duo Nova Air Fryer Lid and select the Broil Smart Program.
4. Set the timer for 10 minutes at the same temperature.
5. Divide into equal portions and serve.

Nutritional value per serving:

Calories: 182kcal, Fat: 3g, Carbs: 8g, Protein: 3g

Chicken, Beans, Corn and Quinoa Casserole

This isn't your regular casserole. The recipe is designed for people who enjoy beans in their quinoa casserole.

Prep time and cooking time: 40 minutes | Serves: 8

Ingredients To Use:

- 1 cup of quinoa, cooked
- 3 cup of shredded chicken breast, cooked
- 14 ounces of canned black beans
- 12 ounces of corn
- 1/2 cup of chopped cilantro
- 6 kale leaves, chopped
- 1/2 cup of chopped green onions
- 1 cup of clean tomato sauce
- 1 cup of clean salsa
- 2 tsp. chili powder
- 2 tsp. of ground cumin
- 3 cups of shredded mozzarella cheese
- 1 Tbsp. garlic powder
- Cooking spray
- 2 jalapeno peppers, chopped

Step-by-Step Directions to Cook It:

1. Lightly grease an oven-safe baking dish with the cooking spray.
2. To the dish, add the chicken, beans, kale, cilantro, green onions, cumin, quinoa, corn, salsa, garlic, chili powder, mozzarella, and jalapenos. Toss.
3. Transfer the baking dish to the Instant Pot cooker base and cover with the Instant Pot Duo Nova Air Fryer Lid.
4. Select the Bake Smart Program and set the timer for 15 minutes at 350°F

Nutritional value per serving:

Calories: 365kcal, Fat: 12g, Carbs: 22g, Protein: 26g

Green Beans Side Dish

The green beans are seasoned and then air fried to give a crispy and delicious taste. This recipe is truly a marvel.

Prep time and cooking time: 35 minutes | Serves: 4

Ingredients To Use:

- 1-1/2 pound of trimmed green beans, steamed for 3 minutes
- Salt and black pepper, as desired
- 1/2 pound of chopped shallots
- 1/4 cup of toasted almonds
- 2 Tbsp. olive oil

Step-by-Step Directions to Cook It:

1. Mix the green beans, pepper, salt, shallots, oil, and almonds in the air fryer's basket. Toss well.
2. Transfer to the air fryer and cover with the Instant Pot Duo Nova Air Fryer Lid.
3. Select the Air Fry Smart Program and set the timer for 2 minutes at 400°F.
4. Divide into equal portions and serve.

Nutritional value per serving:

Calories: 152kcal, Fat: 3g, Carbs: 7g, Protein: 4g

Cod Fillets and Peas

The cod is well-seasoned and then air-roasted to produce a tasty, crunchy, and exquisite meal.

Prep time and cooking time: 20 minutes | Serves: 4

Ingredients To Use:

- 4 boneless cod fillets
- 2 Tbsp. of chopped parsley
- 2 cups of peas
- 4 Tbsp. wine
- 1/2 tsp. of dried oregano
- 1/2 tsp. sweet paprika
- 2 garlic cloves, grated
- Salt and pepper, as desired

Step-by-Step Directions to Cook It:

1. Add the garlic, parsley, oregano, salt, paprika, wine and black pepper to the food processor and pulse until a smooth mixture is obtained. This will serve as the rub
2. Coat the cod with the rub and place in the Instant Pot cooker base. Cover with the Instant Pot Duo Nova Air Fryer Lid and select the Roast Smart Program.
3. Set the timer for 10 minutes at 360°F.
4. When ready, remove the fish and set it aside.
5. Add the pea to the now-empty Instant Pot cooker base and cover with water. Season with salt and cover with the Instant Pot Duo Nova Air Fryer Lid.
6. Select the broil Smart Program and set the timer to 10 minutes at the same temperature.
7. Serve the fish with the peas and drizzle with the leftover rub

Nutritional value per serving:

Calories: 261kcal, Fat: 8g, Carbs: 20g, Protein: 22g

Ham and Eggs

If you have never tried to eat bread and ham together, you definitely don't know what you're missing. The bread is soaked with the egg, and this gives it a delicious hard, and crunchy taste when it is ready. Try this recipe out ASAP!

Prep time and cooking time: 24 minutes | Serves: 1

Ingredients To Use:

- 2 bread slices
- 1 egg white
- 1/2 lb. ham, sliced
- 1 tsp. sugar
- Salt and black pepper, as desired

Step-by-Step Directions to Cook It:

1. Arrange the bread slices together and slice them diagonally.
2. Whisk the egg white in a bowl and add the sugar.
3. Add the bread triangles in the bowl and allow them to absorb the egg mixture.
4. Transfer the coated bread to the air fryer basket.
5. Season the ham with salt and pepper, then transfer to the bottom of the air fryer.
6. Cover with the Instant Pot Duo Nova Air Fryer Lid and select the Bake Smart Program for 24 minutes at 320°F.
7. Turn the bread triangles halfway for an even cook.
8. Transfer the bread and ham into plates and serve.

Nutritional value per serving:

Calories: 89kcal, Fat: 8g, Carbs: 11g, Protein: 7g

Egg White Chips

This recipe can be described in three powerful words –easy, delicious, and fast.

Prep time and cooking time: 15 minutes | Serves: 2

Ingredients To Use:

- 1/2 Tbsp. water
- 2 Tbsp. parmesan, shredded
- 4 eggs whites
- Salt and black pepper, as desired

Step-by-Step Directions to Cook It:

1. Whisk the egg whites in a bowl, then add the salt, black pepper, and water.
2. Scoop the mixture to a pre-prepared muffin pan and transfer it to the air fryer.
3. Cover with the Instant Pot Duo Nova Air Fryer Lid and select the Bake Smart Program. Set the timer for 8 minutes at 350°F
4. Transfer to plates and serve

Nutritional value per serving:

Calories: 180kcal, Fat: 2g, Carbs: 12g, Protein: 7g

Scrambled Eggs

Who doesn't love a good scrambled egg recipe? The spices used in this recipe are not regular, neither is the appliance used for cooking it. Try it out now to experience the extraordinary taste.

Prep time and cooking time: 10 minutes | Serves: 2

Ingredients To Use:

- 2 large eggs
- 2 Tbsp. butter
- Green onions, as desired
- Salt and black pepper, as desired
- 1 red bell pepper, chopped
- A pinch of sweet paprika

Step-by-Step Directions to Cook It:

1. Mix the eggs, paprika, salt, black pepper, bell pepper, and green onions in a bowl.
2. Preheat the Instant Pot cooker base to 140°F and melt the butter.
3. Cover with the Instant Pot Duo Nova Air Fryer Lid, select the Air Fry Smart Program and set the timer for 6 minutes at the 140°F.
4. Scrape the eggs from the air fryer and serve.

Nutritional value per serving:

Calories: 200kcal, Fat: 4g, Carbs: 10g, Protein: 3g

Fast Eggs and Tomatoes

You can have this meal on your plate within 10 minutes. It is fast, it is easy, and it is worth all the fuss.

Prep time and cooking time: 15 minutes | Serves: 4

Ingredients To Use:

- 4 large eggs
- 2 ounces of milk
- 2 Tbsp. of grated parmesan, grated
- Cooking spray
- Salt and black pepper, as desired
- 8 cherry tomatoes, halved

Step-by-Step Directions to Cook It:

1. Lightly grease the Instant Pot cooker base with the cooking spray and preheat to 200°F.
2. Mix the eggs, cheese, salt, pepper, and milk in a bowl.
3. Transfer the egg mixture to the preheated air fryer and cover it with the Instant Pot Duo Nova Air Fryer Lid.
4. Select the Bake Smart program and set the timer for 6 minutes at the same temperature.
5. Add the tomatoes to the air fryer and cook for another 3 minutes.
6. Divide into equal portions and serve.

Nutritional value per serving:

Calories: 200kcal, Fat: 4g, Carbs: 12g, Protein: 3g

Egg White Omelettes

Without the yolk and with the addition of the skimmed milk, the omelets are pure white and delicious.

Prep time and cooking time: 25 minutes | Serves: 4

Ingredients To Use:

- 1 cup of egg whites
- 1/4 cup of chopped tomato
- 2 Tbsp. of skimmed milk
- 1/4 cup of green onions, chopped
- 2 Tbsp. of chopped chives
- Salt and black pepper, as desired

Step-by-Step Directions to Cook It:

1. Mix the egg whites, milk, tomato, onions, chives, salt, and black pepper in the Instant Pot cooker base.
2. Cover with the Instant Pot Duo Nova Air Fryer Lid and select the Bake Smart Program.
3. Cook for 15 minutes at 320°F.
4. Allow to cool, then slice and serve into plates.

Nutritional value per serving:

Calories: 100kcal, Fat: 3g, Carbs: 7g, Protein: 4g

Lunch Egg Rolls

This is an egg roll recipe with an advanced degree. Try it out now to experience the burst of flavor that comes with baking vegetables and eggs together.

Prep time and cooking time: 25 minutes | Serves: 4

Ingredients To Use:

- 1/2 cup of chopped mushrooms
- 1/2 cup of carrots, grated
- 1/2 cup of grated zucchini
- 2 green onions, sliced
- 2 Tbsp. soy sauce
- 8 egg roll wrappers
- 1 egg, beaten
- 1 Tbsp. cornstarch

Step-by-Step Directions to Cook It:

1. Mix the carrots, zucchini, mushrooms, soy sauce, and onions in a bowl.
2. Place the egg wrappers on a flat surface and arrange the veggie mix in them. Afterward, roll the wrappers.
3. Mix the cornstarch and egg in a bowl and use it to coat the egg wrappers.
4. Seal the edges of the wrapper and transfer them to the Instant Pot cooker base.
5. Cover with the Instant Pot Duo Nova Air Fryer Lid and select the Bake Smart Program and set the timer for 15 minutes at 370°F
6. Transfer to a platter and serve.

Nutritional value per serving:

Calories: 172kcal, Fat: 6g, Carbs: 8g, Protein: 7g

Chapter 11: Vegetarian Recipes

Instant Air Fried Potato Chips

The beauty of air fry with the Instant Pot Duo Nova Air Fryer Lid is that you get to fry with 70% less oil. Check out this potato chips recipe air-fried with just 1 Tablespoon of oil.

Prep time and cooking time: 60 minutes | Serves: 4

Ingredients To Use:

- 4 potatoes, slice into thin strips and soaked for 30 minutes, then drained and patted dry with a paper towel
- Salt, as desired
- 1 Tbsp. of olive oil
- 2 tsp. of chopped rosemary

Step-by-Step Directions to Cook It:

1. Mix the potato chips, salt, and oil in a bowl.
2. Transfer to the Instant Pot cooker base and cover with the Instant Pot Duo Nova Air Fryer Lid.
3. Select the Air Fry Smart Program and set the timer to 30 minutes at 330°F
4. Divide into equal proportions, sprinkle with rosemary, and serve as a side dish

Nutritional value per serving:

Calories: 200kcal, Fat: 4g, Carbs: 14g, Protein: 5g

Delicious Air Fried Broccoli

Broccoli has a bitter taste, but when it is air-fried with the Instant Pot Duo Nova Air Fryer Lid, it becomes better.

Prep time and cooking time: 30 minutes | Serves: 4

Ingredients To Use:

- 1 Tbsp. of duck fat
- 1 broccoli head, florets removed and set aside
- 3 garlic cloves, grated
- 1/2 lemon, juiced
- 1 Tbsp. sesame seeds

Step-by-Step Directions to Cook It:

1. Set the empty cooker base to Sauté mode and melt the duck fat.
2. Add the broccoli, lemon juice, garlic, and sesame seeds and transfer to the Instant Pot cooker base.
3. Cover with the Instant Pot Duo Nova Air Fryer Lid and select the Air Fry Smart program.
4. Set the timer to 20 minutes at 350°F.
5. Divide into equal proportions and serve.

Nutritional value per serving:

Calories: 132kcal, Fat: 3g, Carbs: 6g, Protein: 4g

Roasted Eggplant

The Instant Pot Duo Nova Air Fryer Lid adds a crunchy flavor to the otherwise average vegetable.

Prep time and cooking time: 30 minutes | Serves: 6

Ingredients To Use:

- 1-1/2 pound of cubed eggplant
- 1 Tbsp. of olive oil
- 1 tsp. of garlic powder
- 1 tsp. onion powder
- 1 tsp. sumac
- 2 tsp. zaatar
- 1/2 lemon, juice
- 2 bay leaves

Step-by-Step Directions to Cook It:

1. Mix the eggplants, oil, garlic, sumac, onion, zaatar, bay leaves, and lemon juice in the inner pot of the air fryer.
2. Cover with the Instant Pot Duo Nova Air Fryer Lid and select the Roast Smart Program.
3. Set the timer for 20 minutes at 370°F.
4. Divide into equal proportions and serve.

Nutritional value per serving:

Calories: 172kcal, Fat: 4g, Carbs: 12g, Protein: 3g

Glazed Beets

Regular beets are healthy and delicious, but when prepared with the Instant Pot Duo Nova Air Fryer Lid, the taste is transformed, and it becomes extraordinary.

Prep time and cooking time: 50 minutes | Serves: 8

Ingredients To Use:

- 3 pounds of trimmed small beets
- 4 Tbsp. maple syrup
- 1 Tbsp. duck fat

Step-by-Step Directions to Cook It:

1. Set the empty cooker base to Sauté mode and melt the duck fat.
2. Add the maple syrup and beets to the air fryer and cover with the Instant Pot Duo Nova Air Fryer Lid.
3. Select the Air Fry Smart Program and set the timer to 40 minutes at 350°F.
4. Divide into equal proportions and serve.

Nutritional value per serving:

Calories: 121kcal, Fat: 3g, Carbs: 3g, Protein: 4g

Vermouth Mushrooms

Air fried mushrooms can be eaten as a snack or side dish.

Prep time and cooking time: 35 minutes | Serves: 4

Ingredients To Use:

- 1 Tbsp. olive oil
- 2 pounds of white mushrooms
- 2 Tbsp. of white vermouth
- 2 tsp. of herbs de Provence
- 2 garlic cloves, grated

Step-by-Step Directions to Cook It:

1. Mix the mushrooms, oil, herbs de Provence, and garlic in a small bowl.
2. Transfer to the Instant Pot cooker base and cover with the Instant Pot Duo Nova Air Fryer Lid.
3. Select the Air Fry Smart Program and set the timer to 20 minutes at 350°F.
4. Add the vermouth and cook for another 5 minutes.
5. Divide into equal portions and serve.

Nutritional value per serving:

Calories: 121kcal, Fat: 2g, Carbs: 7g, Protein: 4g

Roasted Peppers

Roasted bell peppers can be eaten as a side dish. The slices are crispy and crunchy. Try the recipe out now.

Prep time and cooking time: 30 minutes | Serves: 4

Ingredients To Use:

- 1 Tbsp. sweet paprika
- 1 Tbsp. olive oil
- 4 red bell peppers, chopped into strips
- 4 green bell peppers, cut into strips
- 4 yellow bell peppers, cut into strips
- 1 yellow onion, sliced
- Salt and black pepper, as desired

Step-by-Step Directions to Cook It:

1. Add the all the bell peppers to the Instant Pot cooker base.
2. Add the oil, onion, paprika, salt, and black pepper and cover with the Instant Pot Duo Nova Air Fryer Lid.
3. Select the Roast Smart program and set the timer to 20 minutes at 350°F
4. Divide into equal proportions and serve.

Nutritional value per serving:

Calories: 142kcal, Fat: 4g, Carbs: 7g, Protein: 4g

Creamy Brussels Sprouts and Ham

The cream and spices improve the taste of the broccoli, and the ham adds flavor to the meal.

Prep time and cooking time: 35 minutes | Serves: 8

Ingredients To Use:

- 3 pounds Brussels sprouts, halved
- 1 cup of milk
- A drizzle of olive oil
- 1 pound of chopped bacon
- Salt and black pepper, as desired
- 4 Tbsp. butter
- 3 shallots, coarsely chopped
- 2 cups of heavy cream
- 1/4 tsp. of ground nutmeg
- 3 Tbsp. of prepared horseradish

Step-by-Step Directions to Cook It:

1. Preheat the Instant Pot cooker base to 370°F and add the oil, Brussels, bacon, salt, and black pepper. Toss.
2. Add the shallots, butter, heavy cream, nutmeg, horseradish, milk, and cook for another 25 minutes.
3. Divide into equal proportions and serve.

Nutritional value per serving:

Calories: 214kcal, Fat: 5g, Carbs: 12g, Protein: 5g

Garlic Potatoes

The potato is seasoned with numerous spices and cooked until it is soft enough to melt in the mouth.

Prep time and cooking time: 30 minutes | Serves: 6

Ingredients To Use:

- 2 Tbsp. of chopped parsley
- 5 garlic cloves, grated
- 1/2 tsp. of dried basil
- 1/2 tsp. of dried oregano
- 3 pounds of halved red potatoes
- 1 tsp. of dried thyme
- 2 tsp. of olive oil
- Salt and black pepper, as desired
- 2 Tbsp. of butter
- 1/3 cup of grated parmesan

Step-by-Step Directions to Cook It:

1. Mix the potato, parsley, garlic, oregano, thyme, salt, black pepper, basil, oil, and butter. Toss
2. Transfer to the Instant Pot cooker base and cover with the Instant Pot Duo Nova Air Fryer Lid.
3. Select the Bake Smart Program and set the timer to 20 minutes at 400°F.
4. Sprinkle with the grated parmesan and divide into equal portions.
5. Serve.

Nutritional value per serving:

Calories: 162kcal, Fat: 5g, Carbs: 7g, Protein: 5g

Chapter 12: Snacks and Desserts

Sweet Potato Cheesecake

If you think strawberry cheesecake is the best, then you haven't tried this lovely potato cheesecake cooked with the Instant Pot Duo Nova Air Fryer Lid.

Prep time and cooking time: 15 minutes | Serves: 4

Ingredients To Use:

- 4 Tbsp. of melted butter
- 6 ounces of soft mascarpone
- 8 ounces of soft cream cheese
- 2/3 cup of crumbled graham crackers
- 3/4 cup of milk
- 1 tsp. vanilla extract
- 2/3 cup of sweet potato puree
- 1/4 tsp. cinnamon powder

Step-by-Step Directions to Cook It:

1. Mix the butter and crackers in a small bowl. Press the mixture to the bottom of a cake pan that fits the Instant Pot cooker base. Refrigerate for a few minutes.
2. In a separate bowl, mix the cheese, potato puree, cinnamon, milk, vanilla, and mascarpone. Whisk until well-combined.
3. Spread the cinnamon mixture on the crust and transfer to the Instant Pot cooker base. Cover with the Instant Pot Duo Nova Air Fryer Lid and select the Bake Smart Program.
4. Set the timer to 4 minutes at 300°F.
5. Keep in the refrigerator for a few minutes before serving.

Nutritional value per serving:

Calories: 172kcal, Fat: 4g, Carbs: 8g, Protein: 3g

Cashew Bars

The bars are delicious and yummy. Try this recipe out now with the Instant Pot Duo Nova Air Fryer Lid

Prep time and cooking time: 25 minutes | Serves: 6

Ingredients To Use:

- 1/3 cup of honey
- 1/4 cup of almond meal
- 1 Tbsp. almond butter
- 1-1/2 cup of cashews, chopped
- 4 dates, chopped
- 3/4 cup of coconut, shredded
- 1 Tbsp. chia seeds

Step-by-Step Directions to Cook It:

1. Mix the almond meal, almond butter, and honey in a bowl.
2. Add the coconut, cashews, dates, and chia seeds.
3. Spread the almond mix on a lined baking sheet that is appropriate for the Instant Pot cooker base and cover with the Instant Pot Duo Nova Air Fryer Lid. Press well.
4. Set the timer for 15 minutes at 300°F.
5. Allow to cool, cut into medium bars, and serve.

Nutritional value per serving:

Calories: 121kcal, Fat: 4g, Carbs: 5g, Protein: 6g

Mandarin Pudding

This is a lovely delicacy that is common in South Asia. Let the pudding speak to your taste buds.

Prep time and cooking time: 1 hour | Serves: 8

Ingredients To Use:

- 1 mandarin, peeled and sliced
- 2 mandarins, juiced
- 2 Tbsp. of brown sugar
- 4 ounces of soft butter
- 2 eggs, beaten
- 3/4 cup of sugar
- 3/4 cup white flour
- 3/4 cup of ground almonds
- Honey, for garnish

Step-by-Step Directions to Cook It:

1. Lightly grease an oven-safe loaf pan with some soft butter and sprinkle with brown sugar.
2. Arrange the mandarin slices on the pan.
3. Mix the rest of the butter with the eggs, sugar, almonds, mandarin juice, and flour. Pour this over the mandarin slices in the pan.
4. Cover with the Instant Pot Duo Nova Air Fryer Lid and select the Bake smart Program. Set the timer to 40 minutes at 360°F.
5. Transfer to a plate and drizzle with honey. Serve.

Nutritional value per serving:

Calories: 200kcal, Fat: 5g, Carbs: 8g, Protein: 6g

Sweet Squares

If you have a sweet tooth, then this recipe is perfect for you. It has all the right ingredients in an excellent combination.

Prep time and cooking time: 40 minutes | Serves: 6

Ingredients To Use:

- 1 cup of flour
- 1/2 cup of soft butter
- 1 cup of sugar
- 1/4 cup of powdered sugar
- 2 tsp. lemon peel, grated
- 2 Tbsp. lemon juice
- 2 eggs, whisked
- 1/2 tsp. baking powder

Step-by-Step Directions to Cook It:

1. Mix the flour, sugar, and butter in a medium bowl.
2. Press the mixture to the bottom of a springform pan that fits the Instant Pot cooker base.
3. Cover with the Instant Pot Duo Nova Air Fryer Lid and select the Bake Smart Program.
4. Set the timer to 14 minutes at 350°F.
5. In a separate bowl, mix the sugar, lemon juice and peel, eggs, and baking powder with an electric mixer. Spread this mix over the crust in the pan.
6. Cover with the Instant Pot Duo Nova Air Fryer Lid and bake for another 15 minutes.
7. Allow to cool, then cut into squares and serve.

Nutritional value per serving:

Calories: 100kcal, Fat: 4g, Carbs: 12g, Protein: 1g

Figs and Coconut Butter Mix

Coconut makes everything better. This coconut and fig recipe is a delicacy fit for kings. Serve as a dessert after the main meal.

Prep time and cooking time: 10 minutes | Serves: 3

Ingredients To Use:

- 2 Tbsp. coconut butter
- 12 figs, halved
- 1/4 cup of sugar
- 1 cup of toasted almonds, chopped

Step-by-Step Directions to Cook It:

1. Set the empty cooker base to Sauté mode and melt the butter.
2. Add the almonds, figs, and sugar to the inner pot, then cover with the Instant Pot Duo Nova Air Fryer Lid.
3. Select the Bake Smart program and set the timer for 4 minutes at 300°F.
4. Divide into equal portions and serve.

Nutritional value per serving:

Calories: 170kcal, Fat: 4g, Carbs: 7g, Protein: 9g

Passion Fruit Pudding

Passion fruit has a tangy tropical taste that reminds you of the beach. This pudding is well-flavored and delicious.

Prep time and cooking time: 50 minutes | Serves: 6

Ingredients To Use:

- 1 cup of Paleo passion fruit curd
- 4 passion fruits, pulp and seeds
- 3 and 1/2 ounces maple syrup
- 3 medium eggs, whisked
- 2 ounces of melted ghee
- 3-1/2 ounces of almond milk
- 1/2 cup of almond flour
- 1/2 tsp. baking powder

Step-by-Step Directions to Cook It:

1. Mix half of the fruit curd with the passion fruit pulp and seeds. Scoop the thoroughly combined mixture into 6 oven-safe ramekins.
2. Mix the whisked eggs, ghee, maple syrup, leftover curd, baking powder, flour, and milk in a bowl. Thoroughly combine and scoop into the ramekins.
3. Introduce the ramekins to the Instant Pot cooker base and cover with the Instant Pot Duo Nova Air Fryer Lid.
4. Select the Bake Smart program and set the timer for 40 minutes at 200°F.
5. Allow pudding to cool and serve.

Nutritional value per serving:

Calories: 430kcal, Fat: 22g, Carbs: 7g, Protein: 8g

Chocolate and Pomegranate Bars

Chocolate is always a treat for everyone, and when you combine it with pomegranate bars, it becomes exquisite.

Prep time and cooking time: 2 hours 10 minutes | Serves: 6

Ingredients To Use:

- 1/2 cup of milk
- 1 tsp. vanilla extract
- 1-1/2 cup of dark chocolate, chopped
- 1/2 cup of chopped almonds
- 1/2 cup of pomegranate seeds

Step-by-Step Directions to Cook It:

1. In a medium pan placed over low heat, boil the milk and chocolate for 5 minutes.
2. Remove from heat and add the vanilla, 1/2 of the pomegranate seeds, and 1/2 of the almond nuts.
3. Pour the mixture into a lined baking pan and sprinkle with salt and the leftover pomegranate and almonds.
4. Cover with the Instant Pot Duo Nova Air Fryer Lid and select the Bake Smart program.
5. Set the timer to 4 minutes at 300°F.
6. Remove and keep in the refrigerator for 2 hours.
7. Serve.

Nutritional value per serving:

Calories: 68kcal, Fat: 1g, Carbs: 6g, Protein: 1g

Blueberry Pudding

An excellent blueberry pudding recipe contains all the ingredients in the right proportion. This recipe is one of those great recipes.

Prep time and cooking time: 35 minutes | Serves: 6

Ingredients To Use:

- 2 cups of flour
- 2 cups of rolled oats
- 8 cups of blueberries
- 1 stick butter, melted
- 1 cup of chopped walnuts
- 3 Tbsp. maple syrup
- 2 Tbsp. of chopped rosemary

Step-by-Step Directions to Cook It:

1. Grease a baking pan and add the blueberries. Set aside.
2. Add the rolled oats, flour, walnuts, butter, rosemary, and maple syrup to the blueberries.
3. Transfer to the Instant Pot cooker base and cover with the Instant Pot Duo Nova Air Fryer Lid.
4. Select the Bake Smart program and set the timer for 25 minutes at 350°F.
5. Allow to cool, then serve.

Nutritional value per serving:

Calories: 150kcal, Fat: 3g, Carbs: 7g, Protein: 4g

Chapter 13: Yogurt and Cake

Tomato Cake

Tomato can also be used as the main ingredient of a cake recipe. Try this recipe out now, and you won't be disappointed.

Prep time and cooking time: 40 minutes | Serves: 4

Ingredients To Use:

- 1-1/2 cups of flour
- 1 tsp. of cinnamon powder
- 1 tsp. of baking powder
- 1 tsp. of baking soda
- 3/4 cup of maple syrup
- 1 cup tomatoes chopped
- 1/2 cup of olive oil
- 2 Tbsp. apple cider vinegar

Step-by-Step Directions to Cook It:

1. Mix the flour, baking powder, cinnamon, baking soda, and maple syrup. Stir.
2. In a separate bowl, mix the olive oil, vinegar, and tomatoes.
3. Combine the two mixtures in a bowl and add to a greased springform pan that fits the Instant Pot cooker base.
4. Cover with the Instant Pot Duo Nova Air Fryer Lid. Select the Bake Smart Program.
5. Set the timer for 30 minutes for 360°F.
6. Allow the cake to cool and serve.

Nutritional value per serving:

Calories: 153kcal, Fat: 2g, Carbs: 25g, Protein: 4g

Tangerine Cake

Spice up your cake with this citrus fruit, and your life will never remain the same.

Prep time and cooking time: 30 minutes | Serves: 8

Ingredients To Use:

- 3/4 cup of sugar
- 2 cups flour
- 1/4 cup olive oil
- 1/2 cup milk
- 1 tsp. cider vinegar
- 1/2 tsp. vanilla extract
- 2 lemons, juiced and zested
- 1 tangerine, juiced and zested
- Tangerine segments, for garnish

Step-by-Step Directions to Cook It:

1. Mix the flour and sugar in a bowl.
2. In a separate bowl, mix the milk, oil, vanilla, vinegar, tangerine juice and zest, lemon juice, and zest. Stir until well-combined.
3. Add the flour to the mixture, then transfer to an oven-safe baking dish.
4. Place in the Instant Pot cooker base and cover with the Instant Pot Duo Nova Air Fryer Lid.
5. Select the Bake Smart Program and set the timer for 20 minutes at 360°F.
6. Serve.

Nutritional value per serving:

Calories: 190kcal, Fat: 1g, Carbs: 4g, Protein: 4g

Cauliflower Cakes

This recipe produces a soft and fluffy cauliflower rice cake. Try it now to enjoy the delicious goodness.

Prep time and cooking time: 20 minutes | Serves: 6

Ingredients To Use:

- 3-1/2 cups of cauliflower rice
- 2 medium eggs
- 1/4 cup of white flour
- 1/2 cup of grated parmesan
- Salt and black pepper, as desired
- Cooking spray

Step-by-Step Directions to Cook It:

1. Season the cauliflower rice with salt and black pepper and remove the excess water.
2. Transfer the rice to another bowl, add the flour, eggs, salt, black pepper, and parmesan. Stir well.
3. Shape the cakes and transfer to the grease Instant Pot cooker base. Cover with the Instant Pot Duo Nova Air Fryer Lid.
4. Select the Bake Smart Program and set the timer to 10 minutes at 400°F. Turn halfway.
5. Serve as a side dish.

Nutritional value per serving:

Calories: 125kcal, Fat: 2g, Carbs: 8g, Protein: 3g

Ricotta and Lemon Cake

Lemon adds a sharp, pleasant aftertaste to this recipe. Try it out now to discover its magic.

Prep time and cooking time: 1 hour 20 minutes | Serves: 4

Ingredients To Use:

- 8 eggs, beaten
- 3 pounds of ricotta cheese
- 1/2 pound of sugar
- 1 lemon, grated and zested
- 1 orange, grated and zested
- Butter

Step-by-Step Directions to Cook It:

1. Mix the eggs, sugar, lemon, orange zest, and cheese in a small bowl. Stir until well-combined.
2. Grease a springform baking pan with the butter and spread the ricotta mix in it.
3. Transfer to the Instant Pot cooker base and cover with the Instant Pot Duo Nova Air Fryer Lid.
4. Select the Bake Smart Program and set the timer for 30 minutes at 390°F
5. Allow the cake to cool before serving.

Nutritional value per serving:

Calories: 110kcal, Fat: 3g, Carbs: 3g, Protein: 4g

Maple Cupcakes

The maple syrup adds a distinctive taste to the apple cake. Every bite of this maple cake recipe comes with a burst of flavor.

Prep time and cooking time: 30 minutes | Serves: 4

Ingredients To Use:

- 4 Tbsp. of butter
- 4 eggs, beaten
- 1/2 cup of pure applesauce
- 2 tsp. of cinnamon powder
- 1 tsp. vanilla extract
- 1/2 apple, cored and chopped
- 4 tsp. of maple syrup
- 3/4 cup of white flour
- 1/2 tsp. of baking powder

Step-by-Step Directions to Cook It:

1. Set the empty cooker base to Sauté mode and melt the butter. Add the applesauce, vanilla, maple syrup, and eggs. Fry for a few minutes, then set aside.
2. Mix the flour, baking powder, cinnamon, and apples in a bowl, then scoop into a cupcake pan.
3. Transfer to the Instant Pot cooker base and cover with the Instant Pot Duo Nova Air Fryer Lid.
4. Select the Bake Smart Recipes and set the timer to 20 minutes and 350°F.
5. Allow the cupcake to cool and transfer to a platter and serve.

Nutritional value per serving:

Calories: 150kcal, Fat: 3g, Carbs: 5g, Protein: 4g

Lime Cheesecake

Lime may be sour but, in this recipe, it brings out the flavor of the coconut cream cheese.

Prep time and cooking time: 4 hours 10 minutes | Serves: 10

Ingredients To Use:

- 2 Tbsp. of melted butter
- 2 tsp. of sugar
- 4 ounces of flour
- 1/4 cup of shredded coconut

Filling Ingredients

- 1 pound of cream cheese
- 1 lime, grated and zested
- 1 lime, juiced
- 2 cups of hot water
- 2 sachets of lime jelly

Step-by-Step Directions to Cook It:

1. Mix the coconut, flour, sugar, and butter in a small bowl. Pour the mixture to the bottom a baking pan and press well.
2. Melt the jelly sachets with hot water until it completely dissolves.
3. Add the cream cheese, dissolved jelly, lime juice, and zest to a bowl and stir well.
4. Pour the cream cheese mix over the crust in the baking pan and transfer to the Instant pot cooker base.
5. Cover with the Instant Pot Duo Nova Air Fryer Lid and select the Bake Smart program. Set the timer for 4 minutes at 300°F.
6. Allow to cool then serve.

Nutritional value per serving:

Calories: 260kcal, Fat: 23g, Carbs: 5g, Protein: 7g

Chapter 14: Slow Cooking Recipes

Seafood Chowder

This special chowder dish is great for the holidays when everyone is too busy to monitor the food. Try it out on hectic days.

Prep time and cooking time: 5 hours | Serves: 8

Ingredients To Use:

- 1 can of cream of potato soup
- 1 can of cream of mushroom soup
- 2-1/2 cup of milk
- 4 medium carrots, chopped
- 1 large onion, chopped
- 2 potatoes, cubed
- 2 celery stalks, chopped
- 1 can of chopped clams, drained
- 1 can of medium shrimp, drained
- 4 ounces of flaked crabmeat
- 5 cooked and crumbled bacon strips

Step-by-Step Directions to Cook It:

1. Add the potato soup, milk, and mushroom soup to the Instant Pot cooker base.
2. Stir in the potatoes, carrots, celery, and onions.

3. Cover with the Dehydration tray and Instant Pot Duo Nova Air Fryer Lid
4. Select the Dehydrate Smart Program and set the timer to 4 hours.
5. After 4 hours, add the shrimp, clams, and crab. Replace the cover and set the timer for 20 minutes.
6. Serve into plates and garnish with bacon.

Nutritional value per serving:

Calories: 124kcal, Fat: 12g, Carbs: 15g, Protein: 9g

Potatoes and Tomatoes Mix

The Instant Pot Duo Nova Air Fryer Lid cooks this meal exquisitely. The potato is soft and just melts in the mouth.

Prep time and cooking time: 3 hours 10 minutes | Serves: 4

Ingredients To Use:

- 1-1/2 pounds of red potatoes, cut into quarters
- 2 Tbsp. olive oil
- 1 pint of cherry tomatoes
- 1 tsp. sweet paprika
- 1 Tbsp. of chopped rosemary
- Salt and black pepper, as desired
- 3 garlic cloves, grated

Step-by-Step Directions to Cook It:

1. Mix the potatoes, tomatoes, paprika, oil, garlic, rosemary, pepper, and salt in a bowl.
2. Transfer the mixture to the Instant Pot cooker base and cover with the broil/dehydration tray and Instant Pot Duo Nova Air Fryer Lid.
3. Select the Dehydrate Smart program and set the timer for 16 minutes at 300°F for 3 hours.
4. Divide into equal portions and serve.

Nutritional value per serving:

Calories: 192kcal, Fat: 4g, Carbs: 30g, Protein: 3g

Slow-Cooked Duck Breasts

The slow cooking will allow the optimal absorption of the spices by the duck. The taste of the meat product with this recipe is out of this world.

Prep time and cooking time: 3 hours | Serves: 2

Ingredients To Use:

- 2 duck breasts
- 1 cup of white wine
- 1/4 cup of soy sauce
- 2 garlic cloves, minced
- 6 tarragon sprigs
- Salt and black pepper, as desired
- 1 tablespoon butter
- 1/4 cup sherry wine

Step-by-Step Directions to Cook It:

1. Mix the duck breasts with the wine, soy, tarragon, garlic, pepper, and salt in a bowl.
2. Transfer the contents of the bowl to the Instant Pot cooker base.
3. Cover with the dehydration tray and Instant Pot Duo Nova Air Fryer Lid.
4. Select the Dehydrate Smart Program and set the timer for 3 hours.
5. Discard the soup and serve the duck into plates.

Nutritional value per serving:

Calories: 475kcal, Fat: 12g, Carbs: 10g, Protein: 48g

Chinese Duck Legs

The time required for cooking this recipe is worth it because the taste of the is exquisite.

Prep time and cooking time: 3 hours 20 minutes | Serves: 2

Ingredients To Use:

- 2 duck legs
- 2 dried chilies, finely chopped
- 1 Tbsp. olive oil
- 2-star anises
- 1 bunch spring onions, chopped
- 4 ginger slices
- 1 Tbsp. oyster sauce
- 1 Tbsp. of soy sauce
- 1 tsp. sesame oil
- 14 ounces of water
- 1 Tbsp. of rice wine

Step-by-Step Directions to Cook It:

1. Set the empty cooker base to Sauté mode and heat the oil. Stir in the chili, star anise, sesame oil, rice wine, oyster sauce, water, and soy sauce—Brown for 6 minutes.
2. Add the spring onions and duck legs. Cover with the dehydration tray and Instant Pot Duo Nova Air Fryer Lid.
3. Select the Dehydrate Smart program and set the timer for 3 hours at 320°F.
4. Divide into equal portions and serve.

Nutritional value per serving:

Calories: 300kcal, Fat: 12g, Carbs: 10g, Protein: 48g

Balsamic Beef

The 4 hours spent cooking allows the beef to absorb the sauce and vinegar. It results in a fantastic meal.

Prep time and cooking time: 4 hours 10 minutes | Serves: 6

Ingredients To Use:

- 1 beef roast
- 1 Tbsp. Worcestershire sauce
- 1/2 cup of balsamic vinegar
- 1 cup of beef stock
- 1 Tbsp. honey
- 1 Tbsp. of soy sauce
- 4 garlic cloves, grated

Step-by-Step Directions to Cook It:

1. In an oven-safe baking dish, add the roast, Worcestershire sauce, vinegar, honey, soy sauce, and garlic.
2. Transfer the dish to the Instant Pot cooker base and cover with the dehydration tray and Instant Pot Duo Nova Air Fryer Lid.
3. Select the Dehydrate Smart Program and set the timer for 4 hours at 300°F
4. Divide into equal portions and serve.

Nutritional value per serving:

Calories: 311kcal, Fat: 7g, Carbs: 20g, Protein: 16g

Chapter 15: Sauté Recipes

New England Haddock Chowder

Haddock's firm meat has a delicate flavor, and this makes it ideal for a fish chowder recipe.

Prep time and cooking time: 30 minutes | Serves: 10

Ingredients To Use:

- 1/2 cup of butter
- 3 medium onions, chopped
- 5 medium potatoes, cubed
- 4 tsp. salt
- 1/2 tsp. of black pepper
- 2 pounds of haddock fillets, divided into portions
- 1 quart of scalded milk
- 12 ounces of evaporated milk

Step-by-Step Directions to Cook It:

1. Set the empty cooker base to Sauté mode and melt 1/4 of the butter. Stir in the onions and brown for about 2 minutes.
2. Add the potatoes, pepper, salt, and 3 cups of boiling water. To with the haddock fillets and cover with the Instant Pot Duo Nova Air Fryer Lid. Select the Broil Smart Program and set the timer to 25 minutes at 350°F.
3. Remove the cover and stir in the evaporated milk, scalded milk, and leftover butter.
4. Season with salt and pepper if desired. Serve.

Nutritional value per serving:

Calories: 173kcal, Fat: 13g, Carbs: 10g, Protein: 9g

Halibut Chowder

The fish used in this recipe can be substituted with salmon or tuna, but the tender chunks of halibut does the magic perfectly.

Prep time and cooking time: 15 minutes | Serves: 8-10

Ingredients To Use:

- 2 Tbsp. butter
- 8 scallions, chopped
- 2 garlic cloves, grated
- 4 cans of cream of potato soup
- 2 cans of cream of mushroom soup
- 4 cups of milk
- 8 ounces of cream cheese, cubed
- 1-1/2 pounds of halibut fillets, cubed
- 1-1/2 cup of frozen sliced carrots
- 1-1/2 cup of frozen corn
- 1/4 tsp. of cayenne pepper

Step-by-Step Directions to Cook It:

1. Set the empty cooker base to Sauté mode and melt the butter. Stir in the scallions and garlic. Fry for about 2 minutes.
2. Add the potato soup, milk, mushroom soup, and cream cheese.
3. Add the carrots, corn, and fish, then cover with the Instant Pot Duo Nova Air Fryer Lid and select the Broil Smart Program. Set the timer for 10 minutes at 350°F.
4. Divide into equal portions and serve. Sprinkle with cayenne pepper if desired

Nutritional value per serving:

Calories: 133kcal, Fat: 10g, Carbs: 14g, Protein: 6g

Filet Mignon and Mushroom Sauce

A classic recipe that can be made right in your home with the Instant Pot Duo Nova Air Fryer Lid.

Prep time and cooking time: 35 minutes | Serves: 4

Ingredients To Use:

- 12 mushrooms, sliced
- 1 shallot, chopped
- 4 fillet mignons
- 2 garlic cloves, minced
- 2 Tbsp. olive oil
- 1/4 cup of Dijon mustard
- 1/4 cup of wine
- 1-1/4 cup of coconut cream
- 2 Tbsp. of chopped parsley
- Salt and black pepper, as desired

Step-by-Step Directions to Cook It:

1. Set the empty cooker base to Sauté mode and heat the oil. Stir in the scallions and garlic—Fry for about 3 minutes.
2. Add the mushrooms and cook for another 4 minutes.
3. Add the wine and boil until it evaporates.
4. Add the mustard, coconut cream, salt, black pepper, and parsley.
5. Cover with the Instant Pot Duo Nova Air Fryer Lid and select the Broil smart Program. Set the timer to 10 minutes at 360°F.
6. Divide into equal portions and serve. Garnish with the mushroom sauce.

Nutritional value per serving:

Calories: 340kcal, Fat: 12g, Carbs: 14g, Protein: 23g

Simple Braised Pork

The steps to make the recipe may be simple, but the taste is definitely not. Try out this recipe to experience a remarkable combination of flavors.

Prep time and cooking time: 80 minutes | Serves: 4

Ingredients To Use:

- 2 pounds of pork loin roast, deboned and cubed
- 4 Tbsp. of melted butter
- Salt and black pepper, as desired
- 2 cup of chicken stock
- 1/2 cup of dry white wine
- 2 garlic cloves, grated
- 1 tsp. of chopped thyme
- 1 thyme spring
- 1 bay leaf
- 1/2 yellow onion, chopped
- 2 Tbsp. white flour
- 1/2 pound of red grapes

Step-by-Step Directions to Cook It:

1. Season the pork with salt and black pepper, coat with 2 tablespoons of the melted butter, then transfer to the Instant Pot cooker base.
2. Cover with the Instant Pot Duo Nova Air Fryer Lid and select the Roast Smart Program. Set the timer to 8 minutes at 370°F.
3. When ready, transfer the contents to a bowl.
4. Set the now empty cooker base to Sauté mode and melt the leftover butter. Stir in the onions and garlic. Fry for about 2 minutes.

5. Add the wine, salt, black pepper, stock, flour, thyme, bay leaf, and stir.
6. Add the roasted pork cubes and toss until well-combined. Then cover with Instant Pot Duo Nova Air Fryer Lid.
7. Set the timer for 30 minutes at 360°F.
8. Divide into equal portions and serve.

Nutritional value per serving:

Calories: 320kcal, Fat: 4g, Carbs: 29g, Protein: 38g

Instant Air-Fried Japanese Duck Breasts

The duck breasts are air-fried to perfection with Instant Pot Duo Nova Air Fryer Lid.

Prep time and cooking time: 30 minutes | Serves: 6

Ingredients To Use:

- 6 boneless duck breasts
- 4 Tbsp. of soy sauce
- 1-1/2 tsp. five-spice powder
- 2 Tbsp. of honey
- Salt and black pepper, as desired
- 20 ounces of chicken stock
- 4 ginger slices
- 4 Tbsp. of hoisin sauce
- 1 tsp. of sesame oil

Step-by-Step Directions to Cook It:

1. Mix the five-spice, soy sauce, black pepper, salt, and honey in a small bowl.
2. Coat the duck breast with the soy mixture and set aside.
3. Set the empty cooker base to Sauté mode and heat the hoisin sauce, sesame oil, and ginger. Cook for 3 minutes. Set aside.
4. Transfer the duck to the now-empty Instant Pot cooker base and cover with the Instant Pot Duo Nova Air Fryer Lid.
5. Select the Air Fry Smart Program and set the timer for 15 minutes at 400°F.
6. Serve the duck into plates and drizzle with the prepared hoisin sauce.

Nutritional value per serving:

Calories: 336kcal, Fat: 12g, Carbs: 25g, Protein: 33g

Conclusion

Now that you have a good idea of what the Instant Pot Duo Nova Air Fryer Lid is all about, it is time to use the knowledge to bring those sumptuous recipes to life. Awaken your inner cooking magic. With the Instant Pot Air Fryer as your magic wand, the possibilities are endless.

Bibidi-Babidi-Delicious Dishes-Boo!

Good Luck!

CPSIA information can be obtained
at www.ICGtesting.com
Printed in the USA
LVHW020051211220
674729LV00011B/478